Dickens
on
theatre

D1369036

'on'

'on'
Published by Hesperus Press Limited
19 Bulstrode Street, London W1U 2JN
www.hesperuspress.com

Foreword © Sir Richard Eyre, 2011
Introduction and notes © Pete Orford, 2011
Selection © Hesperus Press Limited, 2011

This collection first published by Hesperus Press Limited, 2011

Designed and typeset by Fraser Muggeridge studio
Printed in Jordan by Jordan National Press

ISBN: 978-1-84391-617-8

Contents

Foreword

'I've never much enjoyed going to plays. The unreality of painted people standing on a platform saying things they've said to each other for months is more than I can overlook.' That's John Updike, and it is an attitude that is shared by many novelists. For me, of course, Updike misses the point. It's the re-creation that animates the art and makes it unique. Anyway, all art forms are unreal in some sense: they have their formal rules and conventions, novels just as much as paintings. A woman once said to Matisse, 'Surely the arm of this woman is too long?' to which Matisse replied, 'It's not an arm, madam, it's a picture.' Like Updike, she'd missed the point.

Theatre thrives on metaphor. Things stand for things rather than being the thing itself, a room can become a world, a group of characters a whole society. It invokes the astonishment of the unreal, the strange, magnified, proportions which occur naturally in childhood. In the theatre fallibility goes hand in hand with immediacy. It happens in the present tense; it's vulnerable, changeable, maddeningly so sometimes. I like the sense of occasion, the event, the participation in a communal act. That's what Dickens liked as well.

Dickens writes vividly about the experience of theatre-going in *The Amusements of the People*. It's a sympathetic description for the reading classes of the dramatic entertainments enjoyed by the working classes: 'heavily taxed, wholly unassisted by the state, deserted by the gentry, and quite unrecognised as a means of public instruction'. He visits the Victoria Theatre (now known as the Old Vic) and watches plays which are simple moral fables underscored with music – melodramas, in fact. His imagined common man, Joe Whelks, 'is not much of a reader, has no great store of books, no very commodious room to read in, no very decided inclination to read, and no power at all of presenting vividly before his mind's eye what he reads about. But, put Joe in the gallery of the Victoria Theatre; show him doors and windows in the scene that will open and shut, and that people can get in and out of; tell him a story with these aids, and by the help of live men and women dressed up, confiding to him their innermost secrets, in voices audible half a mile off; and Joe will unravel a story through all its entanglements, and sit there a long after midnight as you have anything left to show him.'

It's a description that seems familiar, not of audiences in our contemporary theatres, but of audiences at the movies – at *Star Wars*, say, or *Indiana Jones* or *Avatar*. While Dickens has much fun at the expense of the entertainments on offer to Joe Whelks he never patronises him. Far from it, he makes an argument familiar to anyone who has proselytised for public funding of the arts, that 'There is a range of imagination in most of us, which no amount of steam-engines will satisfy' and that imagination is stimulated by the theatre's demands that the audience enter in an imaginative relationship with the events on stage.

In *Two Views of a Cheap Theatre* he admiringly describes the Britannia Theatre in Hoxton, 'erected on the ruins of an inconvenient old building in less than five months, at a round cost of five-and-twenty thousand pounds' with a capacity of 'two thousand and odd hundreds', with excellent sightlines, superbly equipped, 'spacious, fireproof ways of ingress and egress', well served by attendants, and provided with 'convenient places of refreshment'. And cheap. In short, an ideal popular place of entertainment which presents pantomime and melodrama to one audience on Saturday night, and a tub-thumping evangelical preacher on Sunday evening to an entirely different constituency.

The Victoria and the Britannia theatres were two of many not licensed by the state. There were only three 'legitimate' institutions (those with a royal patent): Covent Garden, Drury Lane and the Haymarket. These were the homes of 'serious' theatre, the only ones permitted to perform spoken drama, which meant largely classical plays, more often than not Shakespeare. Unlike the Victoria Theatre, where the audience was 'squeezed and jammed in, regardless of all discomforts', class demarcation was rigidly enforced, with separate entrances for each section of the house so that wealthy box-holders would not have to share the same entrance as those headed for the benches in the pit or the gallery.

The Covent Garden Theatre was run by Dickens' friend Charles Macready, the great actor who had succeeded Edmund Kean as the dominant star of the London stage. He seems to have been a sensitive and intelligent actor, and as producer he commissioned a number of new plays and staged most of the Shakespeare canon, restoring the original ending to *King Lear* for the first time in over a hundred years. In a (slightly risible) poem honouring him after his death Tennyson said:

Thine is it that the drama did not die.
Nor nicker down to brainless pantomime

In his reviews of *Much Ado About Nothing* and *King Lear*, it is clear that Dickens also admired Macready's refusal to 'nicker down', praising his acting and his staging with affection and undisguised partiality – the sort of critic one craves with unalloyed envy.

It is possible that Dickens took a vicarious pleasure in Macready's success. After all, he had himself tried to be an actor. As a young man he had obtained an audition for Covent Garden and, at least according to him, it was only a bad cold that prevented him from going. That diplomatic illness might speak of self-knowledge – he knew he would never be a good or successful enough actor to satisfy himself or the public. Or he knew enough about acting to know that it requires more than a propensity to show off, more than a knack for dazzling your friends with your stories, and more than a dizzying simulation of self-confidence. However, it never held him back him from performing his work in public and engaging in extensive and elaborate amateur dramatics.

Like many novelists (Henry James, Thomas Hardy, Grahame Greene) to whom it seemed a tantalisingly easy way to make money, Dickens made several attempts to write a successful play. Of his four efforts only one, *The Strange Gentleman*, was a (modest) success, both in London and in New York. Despite this, Dickens disowned it a few years later. *The Village Coquettes* was a transparent attempt to mimic the popular successes of the day: a historical romance, an operetta, and a failure. His third play – *Is She His Wife?* – was a one-act farce about marriage, and his fourth was a satirical comedy written on commission for Macready and rejected by him. After this he renounced the professional theatre, just as Nicholas did in *Nicholas Nickleby*.

Dickens' novels demonstrate why he could not write well for the theatre: they are florid, discursive, reflective, overflowing with descriptive passages and prodigal in their excess of images, their profusion of characters, their galleries of grotesques. None of these attributes lend themselves to writing for the theatre, which is a distilled form of writing in which characters have to be introduced by sleight of hand rather than description, where each action has to follow another in a way that appears inevitable, where everything must appear to have happened rather been engineered – all of which must be achieved by dialogue and action alone.

If Dickens' writing is incompatible with the theatre, film is the opposite. Many if not most of his novels have been successfully translated to the screen. Eisenstein told his students that if they wanted to learn how to write a screenplay they should look at any page of a Dickens novel. It is a paradox, given that his novels should be so filmic, that his characters so frequently seem so 'theatrical', but throughout all his writing it is his empathy with his audience and his sense that life is all performance that radiates with such an alluring heat. Like an actor who needs to keep an eye and an ear on the public even at moments of high passion, Dickens always wants to make contact, to entertain and, above all, to receive the applause that is the actor's reward at the curtain call.

As he says in a speech to raise money for actors in hard times: 'I dare say that the feeling peculiar to a theatre is as well known to everybody here as it is to me, of having for an hour of two quite forgotten the real world, and of coming out into the street with a kind of wonder that it should be so wet, and dark, and cold ... by all these things I entreat you to not go out into Great Queen Street by-and-by, without saying that you have done something for this fleeting fairyland, which has done so much for us.' Dickens' unaffected admiration infuses all the pieces in this book.

– Richard Eyre, 2011

Introduction

It is 1832, and Charles Dickens is going to be an actor. As a young man of twenty with dreams of the stage, his application to the stage manager George Bartley is reciprocated with an invitation to audition before him and the actor Charles Kemble at Covent Garden Theatre. However, on the fateful day, illness prevents young Dickens from attending. Given that he will now proceed to become the most popular English novelist of all time, that missed audition will prove to be a pretty good career move. But his fascination and interaction with the theatre does not diminish, and through his writing he will continue to convey and share that enthusiasm with the reader.

Dickens' relationship with the theatre took a number of forms; though he never turned professional, he continued his dreams of acting through amateur performances in a number of contemporary and classic plays. The most obvious impact of these was during the now infamous performance of Wilkie Collins' *The Frozen Deep* through which he met his alleged mistress Ellen Ternan, but in addition to this prominent bearing on his private life, it is fair to say that all of his dramatic ventures would prove a key influence on his writing. His experience of acting was an integral part of his creative process; he often rehearsed characters' speeches aloud when writing his novels, and it has been argued persuasively that Dickens' later forays on the stage for his public readings were as much about acting, if not more so, as simply reading from the page. Dickens' writing style was perfectly suited to dramatic performance, and the page was simply another stage for him. His successful reading tours were effectively one-man dramas that electrified audiences, and drew upon Dickens' long-researched observations and understanding of the stage.

But ultimately Dickens' most vibrant connection to the stage was as an audience member. He visited the theatre regularly, as will become evident from the articles in this collection, and when he edited the memoirs of Joseph Grimaldi, Dickens freely confessed his 'strong veneration for clowns' and celebrated the 'ten thousand million delights of a pantomime'. For Dickens, good drama, like good writing, constituted and celebrated what was best about humanity; it not only entertained, but enriched the soul and heightened emotion. Central to this notion was the figure of William Shakespeare. Dickens and his friend John Forster would celebrate Shakespeare's birthday every year, and the bard's works are repeatedly quoted and drawn upon in Dickens' text. King Lear and Cordelia provided the inspiration for Dombey and Flora, for William and Amy Dorrit, and, most famously, for Little Nell and her grandfather. It is not surprising then that Dickens became such firm friends with the celebrated Shakespearean actor William Charles Macready. Macready's revivalist production of *King Lear*, which dismissed the happy ending of Nahum Tate's adaptation and restored the death of Cordelia, proved to be a great influence on *The Old Curiosity Shop*. It is fitting also that Dickens should have chosen to dedicate *Nicholas Nickleby* to Macready, when it contains the stereotypical actor figure of Mr Crummles. Dickens' treatment of the Crummles family is indicative of his response to theatre as a whole, as it oscillates between bemusement and awe, recognising the community of actors whilst lampooning their petty squabbles, and celebrating the majesty of a theatrical performance whilst reporting on backstage politics.

To be certain, Dickens' love for the theatre did not blind him to its absurdities, and in this collection we can see the dual attitudes of Dickens to the sublime and the ridiculous in drama. The opening article, 'The Amusements of the People' (1850) takes great delight in giving account of the bizarre melodramas being acted out in London theatres at the time, and the same tone can be found in 'Astley's' (1835), concerning the theatre of the same name, primarily famous for its circle which allowed horsemanship and circus acts to be shown as well as conventional theatre; in both articles the audience offers Dickens as much source of entertainment as does the play. The vanity of the actor, and the lure of fame, is then explored in 'Private Theatres' (1835), in which Dickens looks at the phenomenon where anyone could pay to be an actor for the night with prices relative to the size of the part. The potential for comedy in amateur performance, surely something Dickens must have been aware of in a self-deprecatory light, is also explored in the excerpt from *Great Expectations* (1861), in which Pip and his friend Hubert visit Pip's old acquaintance Mr Wopsle in his breakthrough performance as Hamlet, and in 'Mrs Joseph Porter' (1834), in which Shakespeare is once more mutilated by the eager yet untalented Gattleton family.

Yet these articles also express an appreciation of theatre, for all its foolery; and in the remaining articles of this collection we can see Dickens' admiration for the theatre truly shine. His reviews and thoughts on Macready offer a personal (and subjective) reaction to the work of his friend, as well as a more wide-reaching viewpoint on the majesty of both Shakespeare and theatre in general. In 'Two Views of a Cheap Theatre' (1860), he compares two nights in the same theatre: on the first, a pantomime and melodrama is shown; on the second, a sermon is preached. It allows Dickens to once again consider the importance of educating the audience as well as entertaining it: the controversial practice of preaching in theatre was condemned by many as compromising the solemnity of the scripture, yet Dickens favoured it as a positive step aimed at educating the lower classes through a readily available medium. Indeed, in this argument Dickens foretells modern reactions to television and its potential for offering informative programming rather than cheap, sordid entertainment, although it is important to recognise that even while preaching this message, Dickens enjoys the many merits of the pantomime and melodrama as much as he does the sermon.

The final selection in this anthology is an assortment of Dickens' speeches to the General Theatrical Fund. Given

Dickens' frequent involvement in a variety of charity work, it is unsurprising that he took an active role in helping actors in need, championing the fund and its efforts for retired actors of all range and popularity. But Dickens' involvement with the fund has secondary roots beyond his quest for social justice, inasmuch as it also reflected his enthusiasm for theatre: his long association with the fund not only allowed him to give something back to the dramatic profession, but to further celebrate what he termed 'the sacred bond of charitable brotherhood' which the stage offered, a brotherhood that he felt very much a part of.

The feeling was reciprocated: Dickens' own works were regularly adapted for the stage by other writers both during his lifetime and after, sometimes before the final chapters of the books themselves had been written. Dickens responded to these adaptations with a mixture of bemusement and horror; on one occasion he rushed to see the actor Fredrick Yates to stop him 'making a greater atrocity than can be helped of my poor Curiosity Shop, which is "done" there on Monday Night', and even after giving advice to Yates and his fellow actors, Dickens' pessimistic summary was that 'The thing may be better than I expect, but I have no faith in it at all'. The production, like many other adaptations, was a success, with good reviews, and the consistent translation of Dickens' works to the stage in his lifetime reveals the shared interests of his readers and the theatre audience; indeed, the shows thrived on the popularity of the books and Dickens' fan-base to boost ticket sales. Moreover, it betrays not only each book's dramatic potential, but their dramatic narrative, replete with moments of pathos, melodrama, caricature, comedy and tragedy characteristic of the nineteenth-century stage. Thus Dickens influenced theatre just as theatre influenced him.

Whether lampooning its more ridiculous aspects, or championing the sublime, Dickens never loses his enthusiasm for theatre; after all, though 'Private Theatre' mocks those 'idiotic donkeys' who eagerly take to the stage, it must be remembered that Dickens himself was just as guilty of dabbling in drama. Furthermore, while he applauded those plays that offered good moral teachings, neither was he dismissive of simple melodramas or circus shows, and the impact they could have upon an audience. The everyman Joe Whelks in 'The Amusements of the People' has few books and less inclination to read, but he absorbs culture through the theatre, and, as Dickens remarks, 'these people have a right to be amused'. Ultimately, for all his sarcastic observations, the simple lure of the theatre could not escape Dickens. In one of his speeches for the General Theatrical Fnd, he reflects on 'the feeling peculiar to a theatre [...] as well known to everybody here as it is to me, of having for an hour or two quite forgotten the real world, and of coming out into the street with a kind of wonder that it should be so wet, and dark, and cold, and full of jostling people and irreconcilable cabs'; while in 'Astley's' he refers to the actors as 'mysterious beings' whom he refuses to think of outside the theatre 'in threadbare attire [and] the comparatively un-wadded costume of everyday life'. This veneration for the wonder, and escapism, of theatre lies at the heart of Dickens' affection for it, and the infectious passion of the actors was nothing compared to that of the audience, within which there formed another brotherhood. Above all, Dickens' writing testifies to how the world of theatre could offer a moment of relief in the drudgery of the workaday life; for a writer so enamoured by the fantastic as Dickens, theatre could never fail to hold his attention.

– *Pete Orford, 2011*

On Theatre

The Amusements of the People

As one half of the world is said not to know how the other half lives, so it may be affirmed that the upper half of the world neither knows nor generally cares how the lower half amuses itself. Believing that it does not care, mainly because it does not know, we purpose occasionally recording a few facts on this subject.

The general character of the lower class of dramatic amusements is a very significant sign of a people, and a very good test of their intellectual condition. We design to make our readers acquainted in the first place with a few of our experiences under this head in the metropolis.

It is probable that nothing will ever root out from among the common people an innate love they have for dramatic entertainment in some form or other. It would be a very doubtful benefit to society, we think, if it could be rooted out. The Polytechnic Institution in Regent Street, where an infinite variety of ingenious models are exhibited and explained, and where lectures comprising a quantity of useful information on many practical subjects are delivered, is a great public benefit and a wonderful place, but we think a people formed entirely in their hours of leisure by Polytechnic Institutions would be an uncomfortable community. We would rather not have to appeal to the generous sympathies of a man of five-and-twenty, in respect of some affliction of which he had no personal experience, who had passed all his holidays, when a boy, among cranks and cogwheels. We should be more disposed to trust him if he had been brought into occasional contact with a Maid and a Magpie; if he had made one or two diversions into the Forest of Bondy; or had even gone the length of a Christmas Pantomime.[1] There is a range of imagination in most of us, which no amount of steam engines will satisfy; and which The-great-exhibition-of-the-works-of-industry-of-all-nations, itself, will probably leave unappeased. The lower we go, the more natural it is that the best-relished provision for this should be found as dramatic entertainments; as at once the most obvious, the least troublesome, and the most real, of all escapes out of the literal world. Joe Whelks, of the New Cut, Lambeth, is not much of a reader, has no great store of books, no very commodious room to read in, no very decided inclination to read, and no power at all of presenting vividly before his mind's eye what he reads about. But put Joe in the gallery of the Victoria Theatre; show him doors and windows in the scene that will open and shut, and that people can get in and out of; tell him a story with these aids, and by the help of live men and women dressed up, confiding to him their innermost secrets, in voices audible half a mile off; and Joe will unravel a story through all its entanglements, and sit there as long after midnight as you have anything left to show him. Accordingly the theatres to which Mr Whelks resorts are always full; and whatever changes of fashion the drama knows elsewhere, it is always fashionable in the New Cut.

The question, then, might not unnaturally arise, one would suppose, whether Mr Whelks' education is at all susceptible of improvement, through the agency of his theatrical tastes. How far it is improved at present, our readers shall judge for themselves.

In affording them the means of doing so, we wish to disclaim any grave imputation on those who are concerned in ministering to the dramatic gratification of Mr Whelks. Heavily taxed, wholly unassisted by the state, deserted by the gentry, and quite unrecognised as a means of public instruction, the higher English Drama has declined. Those who should live to please Mr Whelks, must please Mr Whelks to live. It is not the manager's province to hold the mirror up to nature, but to Mr Whelks – the only person who acknowledges him. If, in like manner, the actor's nature, like the dyer's hand, becomes subdued to what he works in the actor can hardly be blamed for it. He grinds hard at his vocation, is often steeped in direful poverty, and lives, at the best, in a little world of mockeries. It is bad enough to give away a great estate six nights a week, and want a shilling; to preside at imaginary banquets, hungry for a mutton chop; to smack the lips over a tankard of toast and water, and declaim about the mellow produce of the sunny vineyard on the banks of the Rhine; to be a rattling young lover, with the measles at home; and to paint sorrow over with burnt cork and rouge; without being called upon to despise his vocation too. If he can utter the trash to which he is condemned with any relish, so much the better for him, Heaven knows; and peace be with him!

A few weeks ago, we went to one of Mr Whelks' favourite theatres,[2] to see an attractive melodrama called *May Morning, or The Mystery of 1715, and the Murder!* We had an idea that the former of these titles might refer to the month in which either the mystery or the murder happened, but we found it to be the name of the heroine, the pride of Keswick Vale, who was 'called May Morning' (after a common custom among the English peasantry) 'from her bright eyes and merry laugh'. Of this young lady, it may be observed, in passing, that she subsequently sustained every possible calamity of human existence, in a white muslin gown with blue tucks; and that she did every conceivable and inconceivable thing with a pistol, that could anyhow be effected by that description of firearms.

The theatre was extremely full. The prices of admission were, to the boxes, a shilling; to the pit, sixpence; to the gallery, threepence. The gallery was of enormous dimensions (among the company, in the front row, we observed Mr Whelks) and overflowing with occupants. It required no close observation of the attentive faces, rising one above another, to the very door in the roof, and squeezed and jammed in, regardless of all discomforts, even there, to impress a stranger with a sense of its being highly desirable to lose no possible chance of effecting any mental improvement in that great audience.

The company in the pit were not very clean or sweet-savoured, but there were some good-humoured young mechanics among them, with their wives. These were generally accompanied by 'the baby', insomuch that the pit was a perfect nursery. No effect made on the stage was so curious, as the looking down on the quiet faces of these babies fast asleep, after looking up at the staring sea of heads in the gallery. There were a good many cold fried soles in the pit, besides; and a variety of flat stone bottles, of all portable sizes.

The audience in the boxes was of much the same character (babies and fish excepted) as the audience in the pit. A private in the Foot Guards sat in the next box; and a personage who wore pins on his coat instead of buttons, and was in such a damp habit of living as to be quite mouldy, was our nearest neighbour. In several parts of the house we noticed some young pickpockets of our acquaintance; but as they were evidently there as private individuals, and not in their public capacity, we were little disturbed by their presence. For we consider the hours of idleness passed by this class of society as so much gain to society at large; and we do not join in a whimsical sort of lamentation that is generally made over them, when they are found to be unoccupied.

As we made these observations the curtain rose, and we were presently in possession of the following particulars.

Sir George Elmore, a melancholy baronet with every appearance of being in that advanced stage of indigestion in which Mr Morrison's patients usually are when they happen to hear through Mr Moat, of the surprising effect of his Vegetable Pills,[3] was found to be living in a very large castle, in the society of one round table, two chairs, and Captain George Elmore, 'supposed son, the Child of Mystery, and the Man of Crime'. The Captain, in addition to an undutiful habit of bullying his father on all occasions, was a prey to many vices: foremost among which may be mentioned his desertion of his wife, 'Estella de Neva, a Spanish lady', and his determination unlawfully to possess himself of

May Morning; M.M. being then on the eve of marriage to Will Stanmore, a cheerful sailor with very loose legs.

The strongest evidence, at first, of the Captain's being the Child of Mystery and the Man of Crime was deducible from his boots, which, being very high and wide, and apparently made of sticking-plaster, justified the worst theatrical suspicions to his disadvantage. And indeed he presently turned out as ill as could be desired: getting into May Morning's cottage by the window after dark, refusing to 'unhand' May Morning when required to do so by that lady; waking May Morning's only surviving parent, a blind old gentleman with a black ribbon over his eyes, whom we shall call Mr Stars, as his name was stated in the bill thus ******; and showing himself desperately bent on carrying off May Morning by force of arms. Even this was not the worst of the Captain; for, being foiled in his diabolical purpose – temporarily by means of knives and pistols, providentially caught up and directed at him by May Morning, and finally, for the time being, by the advent of Will Stanmore – he caused one Slink, his adherent, to denounce Will Stanmore as a rebel, and got that cheerful mariner carried off, and shut up in prison. At about the same period of the Captain's career, there suddenly appeared in his father's castle a dark complexioned lady of the name of Manuella, 'a Zingara Woman from the Pyrenean Mountains; the Wild Wanderer of the Heath, and the Pronouncer of the Prophecy', who threw the melancholy baronet, his supposed father, into the greatest confusion by asking him what he had upon his conscience, and by pronouncing mysterious rhymes concerning the Child of Mystery and the Man of Crime, to a low trembling of fiddles. Matters were in this state when the theatre resounded with applause, and Mr Whelks fell into a fit of unbounded enthusiasm, consequent on the entrance of 'Michael the Mendicant'.

At first we referred something of the cordiality with which Michael the Mendicant was greeted, to the fact of his being 'made up' with an excessively dirty face, which might create a bond of union between himself and a large majority of the audience. But it soon came out that Michael the Mendicant had been hired in old time by Sir George Elmore, to murder his (Sir George Elmore's) elder brother – which he had done; notwithstanding which little affair of honour, Michael was in reality a very good fellow; quite a tender-hearted man; who, on hearing of the Captain's determination to settle Will Stanmore, cried out, 'What! More bel-ood!' and fell flat – overpowered by his nice sense of humanity. In like manner, in describing that small error of judgment into which he had allowed himself to be tempted by money, this gentleman exclaimed, 'I ster-ruck him down, and fel-ed in er-error!' and further he remarked, with honest pride, 'I have liveder as a beggar – a roadersider vaigerant, but no ker-rime since then has stained these hands!' All these sentiments of the worthy man were hailed with showers of applause; and when, in the excitement of his feelings on one occasion, after a soliloquy, he 'went off' *on his back*, kicking and shuffling along the ground, after the manner of bold spirits in trouble, who object to be taken to the station-house, the cheering was tremendous.

And to see how little harm he had done, after all! Sir George Elmore's elder brother was *not* dead. Not he! He recovered, after this sensitive creature had 'fel-ed in er-error', and, putting a black ribbon over his eyes to disguise himself, went and lived in a modest retirement with his only child. In short, Mr Stars was the identical individual! When Will Stanmore turned out to be the wrongful Sir George Elmore's son, instead of the Child of Mystery and the Man of Crime, who turned out to be Michael's son (a change having been effected, in revenge, by the lady from the Pyrenean Mountains, who became the Wild Wanderer of the Heath, in consequence of the wrongful Sir George Elmore's perfidy to her and desertion of her), Mr Stars went up to the castle, and mentioned to his murdering brother how it was. Mr Stars said it was all right; he bore no malice; he had kept out of the way, in order that his murdering brother (to whose numerous virtues he was no stranger) might enjoy the property; and now he would propose that they should make it up and dine together. The murdering brother immediately consented, embraced the Wild Wanderer, and it is supposedsent instructions to Doctors' Commons for a license to marry her. After which, they were all very comfortable indeed. For it is not much to try to murder your brother for the sake of his property, if you only suborn such a delicate assassin as Michael the Mendicant!

All this did not tend to the satisfaction of the Child of Mystery and Man of Crime, who was so little pleased by the general happiness that he shot Will Stanmore, now joyfully out of prison and going to be married directly to May Morning, and carried off the body, and May Morning to boot, to a lone hut. Here, Will Stanmore, laid out for dead at fifteen minutes past twelve p.m., arose at seventeen minutes past, infinitely fresher than most daisies, and fought two strong men single-handed. However, the Wild Wanderer, arriving with a party of male wild wanderers, who were always at her disposal – and the murdering brother arriving arm-in-arm with Mr Stars – stopped the combat, confounded the Child of Mystery and Man of Crime, and blessed the lovers.

The adventures of *Red Riven the Bandit* concluded the moral lesson of the evening. But, feeling by this time a little fatigued, and believing that we already discerned in the countenance of Mr Whelks a sufficient confusion between right and wrong to last him for one night, we retired: the rather as we intended to meet him, shortly, at another place of dramatic entertainment for the people.

Mr Whelks being much in the habit of recreating himself at a class of theatres called 'saloons', we repaired to one of these, not long ago, on a Monday evening; Monday being a great holiday-night with Mr Whelks and his friends.

The saloon in question[4] is the largest in London (that which is known as 'The Eagle', in City Road, should be excepted from the generic term, as not presenting by any means the same class of entertainment), and is situated not far from Shoreditch Church. It announces 'The People's Theatre', as its second name. The prices of admission are, to the boxes, a shilling; to the pit, six-pence; to the lower gallery, fourpence; to the upper gallery and back seats, threepence. There is no half-price. The opening piece on this occasion was described in the bills as 'The greatest hit of the season, the grand new legendary and traditionary drama, combining supernatural agencies with historical facts, and identifying extraordinary superhuman causes with material, terrific, and powerful effects.' All the queen's horses and all the queen's men could not have drawn Mr Whelks into the place like this description. Strengthened by lithographic representations of the principal superhuman causes, combined with the most popular of the material, terrific and powerful effects, it became irresistible. Consequently, we had already failed, once, in finding six square inches of room within the walls, to stand upon; and when we now paid our money for a little stage box, like a dry shower-bath, we did so in the midst of a stream of people who persisted on paying theirs for other parts of the house in despite of the representations of the money-taker that it was 'very full, everywhere'.

The outer avenues and passages of the People's Theatre bore abundant testimony to the fact of its being frequented by very dirty people. Within, the atmosphere was far from odoriferous.

The place was crammed to excess, in all parts. Among the audience were a very large number of boys and youths, and a great many very young girls grown into bold women before they had well ceased to be children. These last were the worst features of the whole crowd, and were more prominent there than in any other sort of public assembly that we know of, except at a public execution. There was no drink supplied, beyond the contents of the porter-can (magnified in its dimen-sions, perhaps), which may be usually seen traversing the gal-leries of the largest theatres as well as the least, and which was here seen everywhere. Huge ham sandwiches, piled on trays like deals in a timber-yard,[5] were handed about for sale to the hungry; and there was no stint of oranges, cakes, brandy-balls, or other similar refreshments. The theatre was capacious, with a very large capable stage, well lighted, well appointed, and managed in a business-like, orderly manner in all respects; the performances had begun so early as quarter past six, and had been then in progress for three-quarters of an hour.

It was apparent here, as in the theatre we had previously visited, that one of the reasons of its great attractions was its being directly addressed to the common people, in the provision made for their seeing and hearing. Instead of being put away in a dark gap in the roof of an immense building as in our once national theatres, they were here in possession of eligible points of view, and thoroughly able to take in the whole performance. Instead of being at a great disadvantage in comparison with the mass of the audience, they were here *the* audience, for whose accommodation the place was made. We believe this to be one great cause of these speculations. In whatever way the common people are addressed, whether in churches, chapels, schools, lecture rooms, or theatres, to be successfully addressed they must be directly appealed to. No matter how good the feast, they will not come to it on mere sufferance. If, on looking round us, we find that the only things plainly and personally addressed to them, from quack medicines upwards, be bad or very defect- ive things, so much the worse for them and for all of us, and so much the more unjust and absurd the system which has haughtily abandoned a strong ground to such occupation.

We will add that we believe these people have a right to be amused. A great deal, that we consider to be unreasonable, is written and talked about not licensing these places of entertain- ment. We have already intimated that we believe a love of dramatic representations to be an inherent principle in human nature. In most conditions of human life of which we have any knowledge, from the Greeks to the Bosjesmen, some form of dramatic representation has always obtained.* We have a vast respect for county magistrates, and for the lord chamberlain; but we render greater deference to such extensive and immutable experience, and think it will outlive the whole existing court and commission. We would assuredly not bear harder on the four penny theatre, than on the four shilling theatre, or the four guinea theatre; but we would decidedly interpose to turn to some wholesome account the means of instruction which it has at command, and we would make that office of Dramatic Licenser, which, like many other offices, has become a mere piece of court favour and dandy conventionality, a real, responsible, educational trust. We would have it exercise a sound supervision over the lower drama, instead of stopping the career of a real work of art, as it did in the case of Mr Chorley's play at the Surrey Theatre, but a few weeks since, for a sickly point of form.[6]

To return to Mr Whelks. The audience, being able to see and hear, were very attentive. They were so closely packed that they took a little time in settling down after any pause; but otherwise the general disposition was to lose nothing, and to check (in no choice language) any disturber of the business of the scene.

On our arrival, Mr Whelks had already followed Lady Hatton the heroine (whom we faintly recognised as a mutilated theme of the late Thomas Ingoldsby)[7] to the 'Gloomy Dell and Suicide's Tree', where Lady H. had encountered the 'apparition of the dark man of doom', and heard the 'fearful story of the Suicide'. She had also 'signed the compact in her own Blood';

* In the remote interior of Africa, and among the North American Indians, this truth is exemplified in an equally striking manner. Who that saw the four grim, stunted, abject bush-people at the Egyptian Hall – with two natural actors among them out of that number, one a male and the other a female – can forget how something human and imaginative gradually broke out in the little ugly man, when he was roused from crouching over the charcoal fire, into giving a dramatic representation of the tracking of a beast, the shooting of the poisoned arrows, and the creature's death?

beheld 'the Tombs rent asunder'; seen 'skeletons start from their graves, and gibber Mine, mine, for ever!' and undergone all these little experiences (each set forth in a separate line in the bill) in the compass of one act. It was not yet over, indeed, for we had found a remote king of England of the name of 'Enerry', refreshing himself with the spectacle of a dance in a Garden, which was interrupted by the 'thrilling appearance of the Demon'. This 'supernatural cause' (with black eyebrows slanting up into his temples, and red-foil cheekbones) brought the drop-curtain down as we took possession of our shower-bath.

It seemed, on the curtain's going up again, that Lady Hatton had sold herself to the powers of darkness, on very high terms, and was now overtaken by remorse, and by jealousy too; the latter passion being excited by the beautiful Lady Rodolpha, ward to the king. It was to urge Lady Hatton on to the murder of this young female (as well as we could make out, but both we and Mr Whelks found the incidents complicated) that the Demon appeared 'once again in all his terrors'. Lady Hatton had been leading a life of piety, but the Demon was not to have his bargain declared off, in right of any such artifices, and now offered a dagger for the destruction of Rodolpha. Lady Hatton hesitating to accept this trifle from Tartarus, the Demon, for certain subtle reasons of his own, proceeded to entertain her with a view of 'this gloomy courtyard of a convent', and the apparitions of the 'Skeleton Monk', and the 'King of Terrors'. Against these superhuman causes, another superhuman cause, to wit the ghost of Lady H.'s mother, came into play, and greatly confounded the powers of darkness, by waving the 'sacred emblem' over the head of the else devoted Rodolpha, and causing her to sink into the earth. Upon this the Demon, losing his temper, fiercely invited Lady Hatton to 'Behold the tortures of the damned!' and straightaway conveyed her to a 'grand and awful view of Pandemonium, and Lake of Transparent Rolling Fire', whereof, and also of 'Prometheus chained, and the Vulture gnawing at his liver', Mr Whelks was exceedingly derisive.

The Demon still failing, even there, and still finding the ghost of the old lady greatly in his way, exclaimed that these vexations had such a remarkable effect upon his spirit as to 'sear his eyeballs', and that he must go 'deeper down', which he accordingly did. Hereupon it appeared that it was all a dream on Lady Hatton's part, and that she was newly married and uncommonly happy. This put an end to the incongruous heaps of nonsense, and set Mr Whelks applauding mightily; for, except with the lake of transparent rolling fire (which was not half infernal enough for him), Mr Whelks was infinitely contented with the whole of the proceedings.

Ten thousand people, every week, all the year round, are estimated to attend this place of amusement. If it were closed tomorrow – if there were fifty such, and they were all closed tomorrow – the only result would be to cause that to be privately and evasively done which is now publicly done; to render the harm of it much greater, and to exhibit the suppressive power of the law in an oppressive and partial light. The people who now resort here will be amused somewhere. It is of no use to blink that fact, or to make pretences to the contrary. We had far better apply ourselves to improving the character of their amusement. It would not be exacting much, or exacting anything very difficult, to require that the pieces represented in these theatres should have, at least, healthy purpose in them.

To the end that our experiences might not be supposed to be partial or unfortunate, we went, the very next night, to the theatre where we saw *May Morning*, and found Mr Whelks engaged in the study of an 'Original old English Domestic and Romantic Drama', called *Eva the Betrayed, or The Ladye of Lambythe*. We proceed to develop the incidents which gradually unfolded themselves to Mr Whelks' understanding.

One Geoffrey Thornley the younger, on a certain fine morning, married his father's ward, Eva the Betrayed, the Ladye of Lambythe. She had become the betrayed, in right – or in wrong – of designing Geoffrey's machinations; for that corrupt individual, knowing her to be under promise of marriage to Walter More, a young mariner (of whom he was accustomed to make slighting mention as 'a minion'), represented the said More to be no more, and obtained the consent of the too trusting Eva to their immediate union.

Now it came to pass, by a singular coincidence, that on the identical morning of the marriage More came home, and taking a walk about the scenes of his boyhood – a little faded since that time – when he rescued 'Wilbert the Hunchback' from some very rough treatment. This misguided person, in return, immediately fell to abusing his preserver in round terms, giving him to understand that he (the preserved) hated 'manerkind, wither two eckerceptions', one of them being the deceiving Geoffrey, whose retainer he was, and for whom he felt an unconquerable attachment; the other, a relative, whom, in a similar redundancy of emphasis, adapted to the requirements of Mr Whelks, he called his 'assister'. This misanthrope also made the cold-blooded declaration, 'There was a time when I loved my fellow keretures, till they deserpised me. Now, I live only to witness man's disergherace and woman's misery!' In furtherance of this amiable purpose of existence, he directed More to where the bridal procession was coming home from church, and Eva recognised More, and More reproached Eva, and there was a great to-do, and a violent struggling, before certain social villagers who were celebrating the event with morris dances. Eva was borne off in a tearing condition, and the bill very truly observed that the end of that part of the business was 'despair and madness'.

Geoffrey, Geoffrey, why were you already married to another! Why could you not be true to your lawful wife Katherine, instead of deserting her, and leaving her to come tumbling into public houses (on account of weakness) in search of you! You might have known what it would end in, Geoffrey Thornley! You might have known that she would come up to your house on your wedding day with her marriage certificate in her pocket, determined to expose you. You might have known beforehand, as you now very composedly observe, that you would have 'but one course to pursue'. That course clearly is to wind your right hand in Katherine's long hair, wrestle with her, stab her, throw down the body behind the door (cheers from Mr Whelks), and tell the devoted Hunchback to get rid of it. On the devoted Hunchback's finding that it is the body of his 'assister', and taking her marriage certificate from her pocket and denouncing you, of course you have still but one course to pursue, and that is to charge the crime upon him, and have him carried off with all speed into the 'deep and massive dungeons beneath Thornley Hall'.

More having, as he was rather given to boast, 'a goodly vessel on the lordly Thames', had better have gone away with it, weather permitting, than gone after Eva. Naturally, he got carried down to the dungeons, too, for lurking about, and got put into the next dungeon to the Hunchback, then expiring from poison. And there they were, hard and fast, like two wild beasts in dens, trying to get glimpses of each other through the bars, to the unutterable interest of Mr Whelks.

But when the Hunchback made himself known, and when More did the same; and when the Hunchback said he had got the certificate which rendered Eva's marriage illegal; and when More raved to have it given to him, and when the Hunchback (as having some grains of misanthropy in him to the last) persisted in going into his dying agonies in a remote corner of his cage, and took unheard-of trouble not to die anywhere near the bars that were within More's reach; Mr Whelks applauded to the echo. At last the Hunchback was persuaded to stick the certificate on the point of a dagger, and hand it in; and that done, died extremely hard, knocking himself violently about, to the very last gasp, and certainly making the most of all the life that was in him.

Still, More had yet to get out of his den before he could turn this certificate to any account. His first step was to make such a violent uproar as to bring into his presence a certain 'Norman Free Lance' who kept watch and ward over him. His second, to inform this warrior, in the style of the polite letter-writer, that 'circumstances had occurred' rendering it necessary that he should be immediately let out. The warrior declining to submit himself to the force of these circumstances, Mr More proposed to him, as a gentleman and a man of honour, to allow him to step out into the gallery, and there adjust an old feud subsisting between them, by single combat. The unwary Free Lance, consenting to this reasonable proposal, was shot from behind by the comic man, whom he bitterly designated as 'a snipe' for that action, and then died exceedingly game.

All this occurred in one day – the bridal day of the Ladye of Lambythe; and now Mr Whelks concentrated all his energies into a focus, bent forward, looked straight in front of him, and held his breath. For, the night of the eventful day being come, Mr Whelks was admitted to the 'bridal chamber of the Ladye of Lambythe', where he beheld a toilet table, and a particularly large and desolate four-post bedstead. Here the Ladye, having dismissed her bridesmaids, was interrupted in deploring her unhappy fate, by the entrance of her husband; and matters, under these circumstances, were proceeding to very desperate extremities, when the Ladye (by this time aware of the certificate) found a dagger on the dressing table, and said, 'Attempt to enfold me in thy pernicious embrace, and this poignard...' etc. He did attempt it, however, for all that, and he and the Ladye were dragging one another about like wrestlers, when Mr More broke open the door, and entering with the whole domestic establishment and a Middlesex magistrate, took him into custody and claimed his bride.

It is but fair to Mr Whelks to remark on one curious fact in this entertainment. When the situations were very strong indeed, they were very like what some favourite situations in the Italian Opera would be to a profoundly deaf spectator. The despair and madness at the end of the first act, the business of the long hair, and the struggle in the bridal chamber, were as like the conventional passion of the Italian singers, as the orchestra was unlike the opera band, or its 'hurries' unlike the music of the great composers. So do extremes meet; and so is there some hopeful congeniality between what will excite Mr Whelks and what will rouse a duchess.

Astley's

We never see any very large, staring, black Roman capitals, in a book, or shop window, or placarded on a wall, without their immediately recalling to our mind an indistinct and confused recollection of the time when we were first initiated in the mysteries of the alphabet. We almost fancy we see the pin's point following the letter, to impress its form more strongly on our bewildered imagination; and wince involuntarily, as we remember the hard knuckles with which the reverend old lady, who instilled into our mind the first principles of education for nine-pence per week, or ten and sixpence per quarter, was wont to poke our juvenile head occasionally, by way of adjusting the confusion of ideas in which we were generally involved. The same kind of feeling pursues us in many other instances, but there is no place which recalls so strongly our recollections of childhood as Astley's. It was not a 'Royal Amphitheatre' in those days, nor had Ducrow arisen to shed the light of classic taste and portable gas over the sawdust of the circus;[8] but the whole character of the place was the same: the pieces were the same; the clown's jokes were the same; the riding-masters were equally grand; the comic performers equally witty; the tragedians equally hoarse; and the 'highly-trained chargers' equally spirited. Astley's has altered for the better – we have changed for the worse. Our histrionic taste is gone, and with shame we confess that we are far more delighted and amused with the audience than with the pageantry we once so highly appreciated.

We like to watch a regular Astley's party in the Easter or Midsummer holidays – pa and ma, and nine or ten children, varying from five foot six to two foot eleven, from fourteen years of age to four. We had just taken our seat in one of the boxes in the centre of the house the other night, when the next was occupied by just such a party as we should have attempted to describe, had we depicted our *beau idéal* of a group of Astley's visitors. First of all there came three little boys and a little girl, who, in pursuance of pa's directions, issued in a very audible voice from the box door, occupied the front row; then two more little girls were ushered in by a young lady, evidently the governess. Then came three more little boys, dressed like the first, in blue jackets and trousers, with a lay-down shirt-collar; then a child in a braided frock and high state of astonishment, with very large round eyes, opened to their utmost width, was lifted over the seats – a process which occasioned a considerable display of little pink legs. Then came ma and pa, and then the eldest son, a boy of fourteen years old, who was evidently trying to look as if he did not belong to the family. The first five minutes were occupied in taking the shawls off the little girls, and adjusting the bows which ornamented their hair; then it was providentially discovered that one of the little boys was seated behind a pillar and could not see, so the governess was stuck behind the pillar and the boy lifted into her place; then pa drilled the boys, and directed the stowing away of their pocket handkerchiefs, and ma having first nodded and winked to the governess to pull the girls' frocks a little more off their shoulders, stood up to review the little troop – an inspection which appeared to terminate much to her own satisfaction, for she looked with a complacent air at pa, who was standing up at the further end of the seat; and pa returned the glance, and blew his nose very emphatically; and the poor governess peeped out from behind the pillar, and timidly tried to catch ma's eye, with a look expressive of her high admiration of the whole family. Then two of the little boys, who had been discussing the point whether Astley's was more than twice as large as Drury Lane, agreed to refer it to 'George' for his decision; at which 'George', who was no other than the young gentleman before noticed, waxed indignant, and remonstrated in no very gentle terms on the gross impropriety of having his name repeated in so loud a voice at a public place, on which all the children laughed very heartily, and one of the little boys wound up by expressing his opinion, that 'George began to think himself quite a man now', whereupon both pa and ma laughed too; and George (who carried a dress cane and was cultivating whiskers) muttered that 'William always was encouraged in his impertinence;' and assumed a look of profound contempt, which lasted the whole evening.

The play began, and the interest of the little boys knew no bounds; pa was clearly interested too, although he very unsuccessfully endeavoured to look as if he wasn't. As for ma, she was perfectly overcome by the drollery of the principal comedian, and laughed till every one of the immense bows on her ample cap trembled, at which the governess peeped out from behind the pillar again, and whenever she could catch ma's eye, put her handkerchief to her mouth, and appeared, as in duty bound, to be in convulsions of laughter also. Then when the man in the splendid armour vowed to rescue the lady, or perish in the attempt, the little boys applauded vehemently, especially one little fellow who was apparently on a visit to the family, and had been carrying on a child's flirtation the whole evening with a small coquette of twelve years old, who looked like a model of her mamma on a reduced scale; and who, in common with the other little girls (who generally speaking have even more coquettishness about them than much older ones) looked very properly shocked, when the knight's squire kissed the princess's confidential chambermaid. When the scenes in the circle commenced, the children were more delighted than ever; and the wish to see what was going forward, completely conquering pa's dignity, he stood up in the box, and applauded as loudly as any of them. Between each feat of horsemanship, the governess leant across to ma, and retailed the clever remarks of the children on that which had preceded: and ma, in the openness of her heart, offered the governess an acidulated drop, and the governess, gratified to be taken notice of, retired behind her pillar again with a brighter countenance: and the whole party seemed quite happy, except the exquisite in the back of the box, who, being too grand to take any interest in the children, and too insignificant to be taken notice of by anybody else, occupied himself, from time to time, in rubbing the place where the whiskers ought to be, and was completely alone in his glory.

We defy any one who has been to Astley's two or three times, and is consequently capable of appreciating the perseverance with which precisely the same jokes are repeated night after night, and season after season, not to be amused with one part of the performances at least – we mean the scenes in the circle. For ourselves, we know that when the hoop, composed of jets of gas is let down – the curtain drawn up, for the convenience of the half-price on their ejectment from the ring – the orange peel cleared away, and the sawdust shaken, with mathematical precision, into a complete circle – we feel as much enlivened as the youngest child present; and actually join in the laugh which follows the clown's shrill shout of 'Here we are!' just for old acquaintance' sake. Nor can we quite divest ourselves of our old feeling of reverence for the riding-master, who follows the clown with a long whip in his hand, and bows to the audience with graceful dignity. We don't mean any of your second-rate riding-masters in nankeen dressing-gowns with brown frogs,[9] but the regular gentleman-attendant on the principal riders, who always wears a military uniform with a tablecloth inside the breast of the coat, in which costume he forcibly reminds one of a fowl trussed for roasting. He is – but why should we attempt to describe that of which no description can convey an adequate idea? Everybody knows the man, and everybody remembers his polished boots, his graceful demeanour, stiff, as some misjudging persons have in their jealousy considered it, and the splendid head of black hair, parted high on the fore-head, to impart to the countenance an appearance of deep thought and poetic melancholy. His soft and pleasing voice, too, is in perfect unison with his noble bearing, as he humours the clown by indulging in a little badinage; and the striking recollection of his own dignity, with which he exclaims, 'Now, sir, if you please, inquire for Miss Woolford, sir', can never be forgotten. Again, the graceful air with which he introduces Miss Woolford into the arena, and after assisting her to the saddle, follows her fairy courser round the circle, can never fail to create a deep impression in the bosom of every female servant present.

When Miss Woolford, and the horse, and the orchestra, all stop together to take breath, he urbanely takes part in some such dialogue as the following (commenced by the clown): 'I say, sir!' – 'Well, sir?' (it's always conducted in the politest manner). 'Did you ever happen to hear I was in the army, sir?' – 'No, sir.' – 'Oh, yes, sir – I can go through my exercise, sir.' – 'Indeed, sir!' – 'Shall I do it now, sir?' – 'If you please, sir, come, sir – make haste' (a cut with the long whip, and 'Ha' done now – 'I don't like it', from the clown). Here the clown throws himself on the ground, and goes through a variety of gymnastic convulsions, doubling himself up, and untying himself again, and making himself look very like a man in the most hopeless extreme of human agony, to the vociferous delight of the gallery, until he is interrupted by a second cut from the long whip, and a request to see 'what Miss Woolford's stopping for?' On which, to the inexpressible delight of the gallery, he exclaims, 'Now, Miss Woolford, what can I come for to go for to fetch, for to bring, for to carry, for to do, for you, ma'am?' On the lady's announcing with a sweet smile that she wants the two flags, they are, with sundry grimaces, procured and handed up; the clown facetiously observing after the performance of the latter ceremony – 'He, he, oh! I say, sir, Miss Woolford knows me; she smiled at me.' Another cut from the whip – a burst from the orchestra – a start from the horse, and round goes Miss Woolford again on her graceful performance, to the delight of every member of the audience, young or old. The next pause affords an opportunity for similar witticisms, the only additional fun being that of the clown making ludicrous grimaces at the riding-master every time his back is turned; and finally quitting the circle by jumping over his head, having previously directed his attention another way.

Did any of our readers ever notice the class of people, who hang about the stage doors of our minor theatres in the day-time? You will rarely pass one of these entrances without seeing a group of three or four men conversing on the pavement, with an indescribable public-house-parlour swagger, and a kind of conscious air peculiar to people of this description. They always seem to think they are exhibiting; the lamps are ever before them. That young fellow in the faded brown coat, and very full light green trousers, pulls down the wristbands of his check shirt, as ostentatiously as if it were of the finest linen, and cocks the white hat of the summer-before-last as knowingly over his right eye, as if it were a purchase of yesterday. Look at the dirty white Berlin gloves, and the cheap silk handkerchief stuck in the bosom of his seedy coat. Is it possible to see him for an instant, and not come to the conclusion that he is the walking gentleman who wears a blue surtout, clean collar, and white trousers, for half an hour, and then shrinks into his worn out scanty clothes; who has to boast night after night of his splendid fortune, with the painful consciousness of a pound a week and his boots to find; to talk of his father's mansion in the country, with a dreary recollection of his own two pair back, in the New Cut; and to be envied and flattered as the favoured lover of a rich heiress, remembering all the while that the ex-dancer at home is in the family way, and out of an engagement? Next to him, perhaps, you will see a thin pale man, with a very long face, in a suit of shining black, thoughtfully knocking that part of his boot which once had a heel, with an ash stick. He is the man who does the heavy business, such as prosy fathers, virtuous servants, curates, landlords, and so forth. By the way, talking of fathers, we should very much like to see some piece in which all the dramatis personae were orphans. Fathers are invariably great nuisances on the stage, and always have to give the hero or heroine a long explanation of what was done before the curtain rose, usually commencing with 'It is now nineteen years, my dear child, since your blessed mother (here the old villain's voice falters) confided you to my charge. You were then an infant', etc., etc. Or else they have to discover, all of a sudden, that somebody whom they have been in constant communication with, during three long acts, without the slightest suspicion, is their own child: in which case they exclaim, 'Ah! what do I see! This bracelet! That smile! These documents! Those eyes! Can I believe my senses? – It must be! – Yes – it is – it is – my child!' – 'My father!' exclaims the child; and they fall into each other's arms, and look over each other's shoulders, and the audience give three distinct rounds of applause.

To return from this digression; we were about to say that these are the sort of people whom you see talking, and attitudinising, outside the stage doors of our minor theatres. At Astley's they are always more numerous than at any other place. There is generally a groom or two sitting on the windowsill, and two or three dirty shabby-genteel men in checked neckerchiefs and sallow linen, lounging about, and carrying, perhaps, under one arm, a pair of stage shoes badly wrapped up in a piece of old newspaper. Some years ago we used to stand looking, openmouthed, at these men, with a feeling of mysterious curiosity, the very recollection of which provokes a smile at the moment we are writing. We could not believe that the beings of light and elegance, in milk-white tunics, salmon-coloured legs, and blue scarves, who flitted on sleek cream-coloured horses before our eyes at night, with all the aid of lights, music, and artificial flowers, could be the pale, dissipated-looking creatures we beheld by day.

We can hardly believe it now. Of the lower class of actors we have seen something, and it requires no great exercise of imagination to identify the walking gentleman with the 'dirty swell', the comic singer with the public house chairman, or the leading tragedian with drunkenness and distress; but these other men are mysterious beings, never seen out of the ring, never beheld but in the costume of gods and sylphs. With the exception of Ducrow, who can scarcely be classed among them, who ever knew a rider at Astley's, or saw him, but on horseback? Can our friend in the military uniform ever appear in threadbare attire, or descend to the comparatively un-wadded costume of every-day life? Impossible! We cannot – we will not – believe it.

Private Theatres

'RICHARD THE THIRD. – DUKE OF GLO'STER 2L.; EARL OF RICHMOND, 1L; DUKE OF BUCKINGHAM, 15S.; CATESBY, 12S.; TRESSEL, 10S. 6D.; LORD STANLEY, 5S.; LORD MAYOR OF LONDON, 2S. 6D.'

Such are the written placards wafered up in the gentlemen's dressing room, or the greenroom (where there is any), at a private theatre; and such are the sums extracted from the shop till, or overcharged in the office expenditure, by the idiotic donkeys who are prevailed upon to pay for permission to exhibit their lamentable ignorance and boobyism on the stage of a private theatre. This they do, in proportion to the scope afforded by the character for the display of their imbecility. For instance, the Duke of Glo'ster's well worth two pounds, because he has it all to himself, must wear a real sword, and what is better still, must draw it several times in the course of the piece. The soliloquies alone are well worth fifteen shillings; then there's the stabbing King Henry[10] – decidedly cheap at three-and-sixpence; that's eighteen-and-sixpence; bullying the coffin-bearers – say eighteen pence, though it's worth much more – that's a pound. Then the love scene with Lady Ann, and the bustle of the fourth act can't be dear at ten shillings more – that's only one pound ten, including the 'off with his head!' – which is sure to bring down the applause: and it is very easy to do – 'Orf with is ed' (very quick and loud; then slow and sneeringly) – 'So much for Bu-u-u-uckingham!' Lay the emphasis on the 'uck'; get yourself gradually into a corner, and work with your right hand, while you're saying it, as if you were feeling your way, and it's sure to do. The tent scene is confessedly worth half a sovereign, and so you have the fight in, gratis, and everybody knows what an effect may be produced by a good combat. One-two-three-four-over;

then, one-two-three-four-under; then thrust; then dodge and slide about; then fall down on one knee; then get up again and stagger. You may keep on doing this, as long as it seems to take – say ten minutes – and then fall down (backwards, if you can manage it without hurting yourself), and die game: nothing like it for producing an effect. They always do it at Astley's and Sadler's Wells; and if they don't know how to do this sort of thing, who in the world does? A small child, or a female in white, increases the interest of a combat materially – indeed, we don't think a regular legitimate terrific broadsword combat could be done without; but it would be rather difficult, and somewhat unusual, to introduce this effect in the last scene of *Richard the Third*; so the only thing to be done, is, just to make the best of a bad bargain, and be as long as possible fighting it out.

The principal patrons of private theatres are dirty boys, low copying-clerks in attorneys' offices, capacious-headed youths from city counting houses; Jews, whose business, as lenders of fancy dresses, is a sure passport to the amateur stage; shop boys who now and then mistake their masters' money for their own; and a choice miscellany of idle vagabonds. The proprietor of a private theatre may be an ex-scene-painter, a low coffee house keeper, a disappointed eighth-rate actor, a Chancery officer, a retired smuggler, or an uncertificated bankrupt. The theatre itself may be in Catherine Street, Strand, the purlieus of the city, the neighbourhood of Gray's Inn Lane, or the vicinity of Sadler's Wells; or it may, perhaps, form the chief nuisance of some shabby street, on the Surrey side of Waterloo Bridge. The lady performers pay nothing for their characters, and it is needless to add, are usually selected from one class of society; and the audiences are necessarily of much the same character as the performers, who receive, in return for their contributions to the management, tickets to the amount of the money they pay.

All the minor theatres in London, especially the lowest, constitute the centre of a little stage-struck neighbourhood. Each of them has an audience exclusively its own, and at any, you will see dropping into the pit at half price, or swaggering into the back of a box, if the price of admission be a reduced one, divers boys of from fifteen to twenty-one years of age, who throw back their coats, and turn up their wristbands, after the portraits of Count D'Orsay, hum tunes and whistle when the curtain is down, by way of persuading the people near them, that they are not at all anxious to have it up again, and speak familiarly of the inferior performers as Bill Such-a-one, and Ned So-and-so, or tell each other how a new piece called *The Unknown Bandit of the Invisible Cavern*, is in rehearsal; how Mister Palmer is to play The Unknown Bandit; how Charley Scarton is to take the part of an English sailor, and fight a broadsword combat with six unknown bandits, at one and the same time (one theatrical sailor is always equal to half a dozen men at least); how Mister Palmer and Charley Scarton are to go through a double hornpipe in fetters in the second act; how the interior of the invisible cavern is to occupy the whole extent of the stage; and other town-surprising theatrical announcements. These are your amateurs – the Richards, Shylocks, Beverleys, and Othellos – the Young Dorntons, Rovers, Captain Absolutes, and Charles Surfaces – of a private theatre.

See them at the neighbouring public house or the theatrical coffee shop! Why, they're the kings of the place, supposing no real performers to be present; and roll about, hats on one side, and arms akimbo, as if they had actually come into possession of eighteen shillings a week, and a share of a ticket night. If one of them does but know an Astley's supernumerary he is a happy fellow. You must have remarked the mingled air of envy and admiration with which the companions of the youth regard him, as he converses familiarly with some mouldy-looking man in the fancy neckerchief, whose partially corked eyebrows, and half-rouged face, testify to the fact of his having just left the stage or the circle.

With the double view of guarding against the discovery of friends or employers, and enhancing the interest of an assumed character, by attaching a high-sounding name to its representative, these geniuses assume fictitious cognomens, which are not the least amusing part of the playbill of a private theatre. Belville, Melville, Treville, Berkeley, Randolph, Byron, St Clair, and so forth, are among the humblest; and the less imposing titles of Jenkins, Walker, Thomson, Barker, Solomons, etc., are completely laid aside. There is something imposing in this, and it is an excellent apology for shabbiness into the bargain. A shrunken, faded coat, a decayed hat, a patched and soiled pair of trousers – nay even a very dirty shirt (and none of these appearances are very uncommon among the members of the *corps dramatique*), may be worn for the purpose of disguise, and to prevent the remotest chance of recognition. Then it prevents any troublesome inquiries or explanations about employment and pursuits; everybody is a gentleman at large for the occasion, and there are none of those unpleasant and unnecessary distinctions to which even genius must occasionally succumb elsewhere. As to the ladies (God bless 'em), they're quite above any formal absurdities; the mere circumstance of your being behind the scenes is a sufficient introduction to their society – for of course they know that none but strictly respectable persons would be admitted into that close fellowship with them which acting engenders. They place implicit reliance on the manager, no doubt; and as to the manager, he is all affability when he knows you well, – or, in other words, when he has pocketed your money once, and entertains confident hopes of doing so again.

A quarter before eight – there will be a full house tonight – six parties in the boxes already, four little boys and a woman in the pit; and two fiddles and a flute in the orchestra, who have got through five overtures since seven o'clock (the hour fixed for the commencement of the performances), and have just begun the sixth. There will be plenty of it, though, when it does begin, for there is enough in the bill to last six hours at least.

That gentleman in the white hat and checked shirt, brown coat and brass buttons, lounging behind the stage box on the

O. P. side,[11] is Mr Horatio St Julien, alias Jem Larkins. His line is genteel comedy – his father's, coal and potato. He does Alfred Highflier in the last piece, and very well he'll do it – at the price. The party of gentlemen in the opposite box, to whom he has just nodded, are friends and supporters of Mr Beverley (otherwise Loggins), the Macbeth of the night. You observe their attempts to appear easy and gentlemanly; each member of the party, with his feet cocked upon the cushion in front of the box! They let 'em do these things here, upon the same humane principle which permits poor people's children to knock double knocks at the door of an empty house – because they can't do it anywhere else. The two stout men in the centre box, with an opera glass ostentatiously placed before them, are friends of the proprietor – opulent country managers, as he confidentially informs every individual among the crew behind the curtain – opulent country managers looking out for recruits; a representation which Mr Nathan, the dresser, who is in the manager's interest, and has just arrived with the costumes, offers to confirm upon oath if required – corroborative evidence, however, is quite unnecessary, for the gulls believe it at once.

The stout Jewess who has just entered is the mother of the pale bony little girl, with the necklace of blue glass beads, sitting by her; she is being brought up to 'the profession'. Pantomime is to be her line, and she is coming out tonight in a hornpipe after the tragedy. The short thin man beside Mr St Julien, whose white face is so deeply seared with the smallpox, and whose dirty shirt front is inlaid with open-work, and embossed with coral studs like ladybirds, is the low comedian and comic singer of the establishment. The remainder of the audience – a tolerably numerous one by this time – are a motley group of dupes and blackguards.

The footlights have just made their appearance: the wicks of the six little oil lamps round the only tier of boxes are being turned up, and the additional light thus afforded serves to show the presence of dirt and absence of paint, which forms a prominent feature in the audience part of the house. As these preparations, however, announce the speedy commencement of the play, let us take a peep behind, previous to the ringing up.

The little narrow passages beneath the stage are neither especially clean, nor too brilliantly lighted; and the absence of any flooring, together with the damp, mildewy smell which pervades the places, does not conduce in any great degree to their comfortable appearance. Don't fall over this plate basket – it's one of the 'properties', the cauldron for the witches' cave; and the three uncouth-looking figures, with broken clothes-props in their hands, who are drinking gin and water out of a pint pot, are the weird sisters. This miserable room, lighted by candles in sconces placed at lengthened intervals round the wall, is the dressing room, common to the gentlemen performers, and the square hole in the ceiling is the trapdoor of the stage above. You will observe that the ceiling is ornamented with the beams that support the boards, and is tastefully hung with cobwebs.

The characters in the tragedy are all dressed, and their own clothes are scattered in hurried confusion over the wooden dresser which surrounds the room. That snuff-shop-looking figure, in front of the glass, is Banquo, and the young lady with the liberal display of legs, who is kindly painting his face with a hare's foot, is dressed for Fleance. The large woman, who is consulting the stage directions in Cumberland's edition of Macbeth, is the Lady Macbeth of the night; she is always selected to play the part, because she is tall and stout, and looks a little like Mrs Siddons[12] – at a considerable distance. That stupid-looking milksop, with light hair and bow legs – a kind of man whom you can warrant townmade – is fresh caught; he plays Malcolm tonight, just to accustom himself to an audience. He will get on better by degrees; he will play Othello in a month, and in a month more, will very probably be apprehended on a charge of embezzlement. The black-eyed female with whom he is talking so earnestly, is dressed for the 'gentlewoman'. It's her first appearance, too – in that character. The boy of fourteen, who is having his eyebrows smeared with soap and whitening, is Duncan, King of Scotland; and the two dirty men with the corked countenances, in very old green tunics, and dirty drab boots, are the 'army'.

'Look sharp below there, gents,' exclaims the dresser, a red-headed and red-whiskered Jew, calling through the trap, 'they're a-going to ring up. The flute says he'll be blowed if he plays any more, and they're getting precious noisy in front.' A general rush immediately takes place to the half-dozen little steep steps leading to the stage, and the heterogeneous group are soon assembled at the side scenes in breathless anxiety and motley confusion.

'Now,' cries the manager, consulting the written list which hangs behind the first P.S. wing,[13] 'Scene 1, open country – lamps down – thunder and lightning – all ready, White?' [this is addressed to one of the army].

'All ready.'

'Very well, scene 2, front chamber; is the front chamber down?'

'Yes.'

'Very well. Jones' [to the other army who is up in the flies].

'Hallo!'

'Wind up the open country when we ring up.'

'I'll take care,' growls the elevated army.

'Scene 3, back perspective with practical bridge. Bridge ready, White? Got the tressels there?'

'All right,' responds the functionary.

'Very well. Clear the stage,' adds the manager, hastily packing every member of the company into the little space there is between the wings and the wall; and one wing and another.

'Places, places, now then, witches – Duncan – Malcolm – bloody officer – where's that bloody officer?'

'Here!' replies the officer, who has been rose-pinking for the character.

'Get ready, then; now, White, ring the second music bell.' The actors who are to be discovered, are hastily arranged, and the actors who are not to be discovered place themselves, in their anxiety to peep at the house, just where the whole audience can see them. The bell rings, and the orchestra, in acknowledgment of the call, play three distinct chords. The bell rings – the tragedy (!) opens – and our description closes.

Mr Wopsle Plays Hamlet

On our arrival in Denmark, we found the king and queen of that country elevated in two armchairs on a kitchen table, holding a court. The whole of the Danish nobility were in attendance; consisting of a noble boy in the wash-leather boots of a gigantic ancestor, a venerable peer with a dirty face who seemed to have risen from the people late in life, and the Danish chivalry with a comb in its hair and a pair of white silk legs, and presenting on the whole a feminine appearance. My gifted townsman stood gloomily apart, with folded arms, and I could have wished that his curls and forehead had been more probable.

Several curious little circumstances transpired as the action proceeded. The late King of the country not only appeared to have been troubled with a cough at the time of his decease, but to have taken it with him to the tomb, and to have brought it back. The royal phantom also carried a ghostly manuscript round its truncheon, to which it had the appearance of occasionally referring, and that, too, with an air of anxiety and a tendency to lose the place of reference which were suggestive of a state of mortality. It was this, I conceive, which led to the shade's being advised by the gallery to 'turn over!' – a recommendation which it took extremely ill. It was likewise to be noted of this majestic spirit that whereas it always appeared with an air of having been out a long time and walked an immense distance, it perceptibly came from a closely contiguous wall. This occasioned its terrors to be received derisively. The Queen of Denmark, a very buxom lady, though no doubt historically brazen, was considered by the public to have too much brass about her; her chin being attached to her diadem by a broad band of that metal (as if she had a gorgeous toothache), her waist being encircled by another, and each of her arms by another, so that she was openly mentioned as 'the kettledrum'. The noble boy in the ancestral boots, was inconsistent; representing himself, as it were in one breath, as an able seaman, a strolling actor, a gravedigger, a clergyman, and a person of the utmost importance at a Court fencing match, on the authority of whose practised eye and nice discrimination the finest strokes were judged. This gradually led to a want of toleration for him, and even – on his being detected in holy orders, and declining to perform the funeral service – to the general indignation taking the form of nuts. Lastly, Ophelia was a prey to such slow musical madness, that when, in course of time, she had taken off her white muslin scarf, folded it up, and buried it, a sulky man who had been long cooling his impatient nose against an iron bar in the front row of the gallery, growled, 'Now the baby's put to bed let's have supper!' Which, to say the least of it, was out of keeping.

Upon my unfortunate townsman all these incidents accumulated with playful effect. Whenever that undecided Prince had to ask a question or state a doubt, the public helped him out with it. As for example; on the question whether 'twas nobler in the mind to suffer, some roared yes, and some no, and some inclining to both opinions said 'toss up for it'; and quite a Debating Society arose. When he asked what should such fellows as he do crawling between earth and heaven, he was encouraged with loud cries of 'Hear, hear!' When he appeared with his stocking disordered (its disorder expressed, according to usage, by one very neat fold in the top, which I suppose to be always got up with a flat iron), a conversation took place in the gallery respecting the paleness of his leg, and whether it was occasioned by the turn the ghost had given him. On his taking the recorders – very like a little black flute that had just been played in the orchestra and handed out at the door – he was called upon unanimously for Rule Britannia. When he recommended the player not to saw the air thus, the sulky man said, 'And don't *you* do it, neither; you're a deal worse than *him*!' And I grieve to add that peals of laughter greeted Mr Wopsle on every one of these occasions.

But his greatest trials were in the churchyard: which had the appearance of a primeval forest, with a kind of small ecclesiastical wash-house on one side, and a turnpike-gate on the other. Mr Wopsle in a comprehensive black cloak, being descried entering at the turnpike, the gravedigger was admonished in a friendly way, 'Look out! Here's the undertaker a coming, to see how you're getting on with your work!' I believe it is well known in a constitutional country that Mr Wopsle could not possibly have returned the skull, after moralising over it, without dusting his fingers on a white napkin taken from his breast; but even that innocent and indispensable action did not pass without the comment 'Wai-ter!' The arrival of the body for interment (in an empty black box with the lid tumbling open), was the signal for a general joy which was much enhanced by the discovery, among the bearers, of an individual obnoxious to identification. The joy attended Mr Wopsle through his struggle with Laertes on the brink of the orchestra and the grave, and slackened no more until he had tumbled the king off the kitchen table, and had died by inches from the ankles upward.

We had made some pale efforts in the beginning to applaud Mr Wopsle; but they were too hopeless to be persisted in. Therefore we had sat, feeling keenly for him, but laughing, nevertheless, from ear to ear. I laughed in spite of myself all the time, the whole thing was so droll; and yet I had a latent impression that there was something decidedly fine in Mr Wopsle's elocution – not for old associations' sake, I am afraid, but because it was very slow, very dreary, very uphill and downhill, and very unlike any way in which any man in any natural circumstances of life or death ever expressed himself about anything. When the tragedy was over, and he had been called for and hooted, I said to Herbert, 'Let us go at once, or perhaps we shall meet him.'

We made all the haste we could downstairs, but we were not quick enough either. Standing at the door was a Jewish man with an unnatural heavy smear of eyebrow, who caught my eyes as we advanced, and said, when we came up with him:

'Mr Pip and friend?'

Identity of Mr Pip and friend confessed.

'Mr Waldengarver,' said the man, 'would be glad to have the honour.'

'Waldengarver?' I repeated – when Herbert murmured in my ear, 'Probably Wopsle.'

'Oh!' said I. 'Yes. Shall we follow you?'

'A few steps, please.' When we were in a side alley, he turned and asked, 'How did you think he looked? – *I* dressed him.'

I don't know what he had looked like, except a funeral; with the addition of a large Danish sun or star hanging round his neck by a blue ribbon, that had given him the appearance of being insured in some extraordinary Fire Office. But I said he had looked very nice.

'When he come to the grave,' said our conductor, 'he showed his cloak beautiful. But, judging from the wing, it looked to me that when he see the ghost in the Queen's apartment, he might have made more of his stockings.'

I modestly assented, and we all fell through a little dirty swing door, into a sort of hot packing case immediately behind it. Here Mr Wopsle was divesting himself of his Danish garments, and here there was just room for us to look at him over one another's shoulders, by keeping the packing case door, or lid, wide open.

'Gentlemen,' said Mr Wopsle, 'I am proud to see you. I hope, Mr Pip, you will excuse my sending round. I had the happiness to know you in former times, and the drama has ever had a claim which has ever been acknowledged, on the noble and the affluent.'

Meanwhile, Mr Waldengarver, in a frightful perspiration, was trying to get himself out of his princely sables.

'Skin the stockings off, Mr Waldengarver,' said the owner of that property, 'or you'll bust 'em. Bust 'em, and you'll bust five-and-thirty shillings. Shakespeare never was complimented with a finer pair. Keep quiet in your chair now, and leave 'em to me.'

With that, he went upon his knees, and began to flay his victim; who, on the first stocking coming off, would certainly have fallen over backward with his chair, but for there being no room to fall anyhow.

I had been afraid until then to say a word about the play. But then, Mr Waldengarver looked up at us complacently, and said:

'Gentlemen, how did it seem to you, to go, in front?'

Herbert said from behind (at the same time poking me), 'capitally'. So I said 'capitally'.

'How did you like my reading of the character, gentlemen?' said Mr Waldengarver, almost, if not quite, with patronage.

Herbert said from behind (again poking me), 'massive and concrete'. So I said boldly, as if I had originated it, and must beg to insist upon it, 'massive and concrete'.

'I am glad to have your approbation, gentlemen,' said Mr Waldengarver, with an air of dignity, in spite of his being ground against the wall at the time, and holding on by the seat of the chair.

'But I'll tell you one thing, Mr Waldengarver,' said the man who was on his knees, 'in which you're out in your reading. Now mind! I don't care who says contrary; I tell you so. You're out in your reading of Hamlet when you get your legs in profile. The last Hamlet as I dressed, made the same mistakes in his reading at rehearsal, till I got him to put a large red wafer on each of his shins, and then at that rehearsal (which was the last) I went in front, sir, to the back of the pit, and whenever his reading brought him into profile, I called out 'I don't see no wafers!' And at night his reading was lovely.'

Mr Waldengarver smiled at me, as much as to say 'a faithful dependent – I overlook his folly'; and then said aloud, 'My view is a little classic and thoughtful for them here; but they will improve, they will improve.'

Herbert and I said together, Oh, no doubt they would improve.

'Did you observe, gentlemen,' said Mr Waldengarver, 'that there was a man in the gallery who endeavoured to cast derision on the service – I mean, the representation?'

We basely replied that we rather thought we had noticed such a man. I added, 'He was drunk, no doubt.'

'Oh dear no, sir,' said Mr Wopsle, 'not drunk. His employer would see to that, sir. His employer would not allow him to be drunk.'

'You know his employer?' said I.

Mr Wopsle shut his eyes, and opened them again; performing both ceremonies very slowly. 'You must have observed, gentlemen,' said he, 'an ignorant and a blatant ass, with a rasping throat and a countenance expressive of low malignity, who went through – I will not say sustained – the rôle (if I may use a French expression) of Claudius King of Denmark. That is his employer, gentlemen. Such is the profession!'

Without distinctly knowing whether I should have been more sorry for Mr Wopsle if he had been in despair, I was so sorry for him as it was, that I took the opportunity of his turning round to have his braces put on – which jostled us out at the doorway – to ask Herbert what he thought of having him home to supper? Herbert said he thought it would be kind to do so; therefore I invited him, and he went to Barnard's with us, wrapped up to the eyes, and we did our best for him, and he sat until two o'clock in the morning, reviewing his success and developing his plans. I forget in detail what they were, but I have a general recollection that he was to begin with reviving the drama, and to end with crushing it; inasmuch as his decease would leave it utterly bereft and without a chance or hope.

Mrs Joseph Porter

Most extensive were the preparations at Rose Villa, Clapham Rise, in the occupation of Mr Gattleton (a stockbroker in especially comfortable circumstances), and great was the anxiety of Mr Gattleton's interesting family, as the day fixed for the representation of the private play which had been 'many months in preparation', approached. The whole family was infected with the mania for private theatricals; the house, usually so clean and tidy, was, to use Mr Gattleton's expressive description, 'regularly turned out o' windows'; the large dining room, dismantled of its furniture and ornaments, presented a strange jumble of flats, flies, wings, lamps, bridges, clouds, thunder and lightning, festoons and flowers, daggers and foil, and all the other messes which in theatrical slang are included under the comprehensive name of 'properties'. The bedrooms were crowded with scenery, the kitchen was occupied by carpenters. Rehearsals took place every other night in the drawing room, and every sofa in the house was more or less damaged by the perseverance and spirit with which Mr Sempronius Gattleton, and Miss Lucina, rehearsed the smothering scene in *Othello* – it having been determined that that tragedy should form the first portion of the evening's entertainments.

'When we're a *leetle* more perfect, I think it will go off admirably,' said Mr Sempronius, addressing his *corps dramatique*, at the conclusion of the hundred and fiftieth rehearsal. In consideration of his sustaining the trifling inconvenience of bearing all the expenses of the play, Mr Sempronius had been in the most handsome manner, unanimously elected stage manager. 'Evans,' continued Mr Gattleton, jun., addressing a tall, thin, pale young gentleman, with extensive whiskers – 'Evans, upon my word you play Roderigo beautifully.'

'Beautifully,' echoed the three Miss Gattletons; for Mr Evans was pronounced by all his lady friends to be 'quite a dear'. He looked so interesting, and had such lovely whiskers, to say nothing of his talent for writing verses in albums and playing the flute! The interesting Roderigo simpered and bowed.

'But I think,' added the manager, 'you are hardly perfect in the – fall – in the fencing scene, where you are – you understand?'

'It's very difficult,' said Mr Evans, thoughtfully; 'I've fallen about a good deal in our counting house lately for practice; only it hurts one so. Being obliged to fall backwards, you see, it bruises one's head a good deal.'

'But you must take care you don't knock a wing down,' said Mr Gattleton, sen., who had been appointed prompter, and who took as much interest in the play as the youngest of the company. 'The stage is very narrow, you know.'

'Oh! don't be afraid,' said Mr Evans, with a very self-satisfied air; 'I shall fall with my head "off", and then I can't do any harm.'

'But, egad,' said the manager, rubbing his hands, 'we shall make a decided hit in *Masaniello*.[14] Harleigh sings that music admirably.'

Everybody echoed the sentiment. Mr Harleigh smiled, and looked foolish – not an unusual thing with him – hummed 'Behold how brightly breaks the morning', and blushed as red as the fisherman's nightcap he was trying on.

'Let's see,' resumed the manager, telling the number on his fingers, 'we shall have three dancing female peasants, besides Fenella, and four fishermen. Then, there's our man Tom; he can have a pair of ducks of mine, and a check shirt of Bob's, and a red nightcap, and he'll do for another – that's five. In the choruses, of course, we can sing at the sides; and in the market scene we can walk about in cloaks and things. When the revolt takes place, Tom must keep rushing in on one side and out on the other, with a pickaxe, as fast as he can. The effect will be electrical; 'twill look just as if there were a great number of 'em: and in the eruption scene we must burn the red fire, and upset the tea trays, and make all sorts of noises – and it's sure to do.'

'Sure! sure!' cried all the performers *una voice* – and away hurried Mr Sempronius Gattleton to wash the burnt cork off his face, and superintend the 'setting up' of some of the amateur painted and never-sufficiently-to-be-admired scenery.

Mrs Gattleton was a kind, good-tempered, vulgar old soul, exceedingly fond of her husband and children, and entertaining only three dislikes. In the first place, she had a natural antipathy to anybody else's unmarried daughters; in the second, she was in bodily fear of anything in the shape of ridicule; and, lastly – almost a necessary consequence of this feeling – she regarded, with feelings of the utmost horror, 'Mrs Joseph Porter, over the way'. However, the good folks of Clapham and its vicinity stood very much in awe of scandal and sarcasm; and thus Mrs Joseph Porter was courted, and flattered, and caressed, and invited, for much the same reason that a poor author without a farthing in his pocket, behaves with the most extraordinary civility to a twopenny postman.

'Never mind, ma,' said Miss Emma Porter, in colloquy with her respected relative, and trying to look unconcerned; 'if they had invited me, you know that neither you nor pa would have allowed me to take part in such an exhibition.'

'Just what I should have thought from your high sense of propriety,' returned the mother, 'I am glad to see, Emma, you know how to designate the proceeding.' Miss P., by-the-by, had only the week before made 'an exhibition' of herself for four days, behind a counter at a fancy fair, to all and every of his Majesty's liege subjects who were disposed to pay a shilling each for the privilege of seeing some four dozen girls flirting with strangers, and playing at shop.

'There!' said Mrs Porter, looking out of the window; 'there are two rounds of beef and a ham going in, clearly for sand-wiches; and Thomas, the pastry cook, says, there have been twelve dozen tarts ordered, besides blancmange and jellies. Upon my word! think of the Miss Gattletons in fancy dresses, too!'

'Oh, it's too ridiculous!' said Miss Porter, with a sort of hysterical chuckle.

'I'll manage to put them a little out of conceit with the business, however,' said Mrs Porter; and out she went on her charitable errand.

'Well, my dear Mrs Gattleton,' said Mrs Joseph Porter – after they had been closeted for some time, and when, by dint of indefatigable pumping, she had managed to extract all the news about the play – 'well, my dear, people may say what they please; indeed we know they will, for some folks are *so* ill natured. Ah, my dear Miss Lucina, how d'ye do? – I was just telling your mamma that I have heard it said, that –'

'What?' inquired the Desdemona.

'Mrs Porter is alluding to the play, my dear,' said Mrs Gattleton; 'she was, I am sorry to say, just informing me that –'

'Oh, now pray don't mention it,' interrupted Mrs Porter; 'it's most absurd – quite as absurd as young What's-his-name saying he wondered how Miss Caroline, with such a foot and ankle, could have the vanity to play Fenella.'

'Highly impertinent, whoever said it,' said Mrs Gattleton, bridling up.

'Certainly, my dear,' chimed in the delighted Mrs Porter; 'most undoubtedly! Because, as I said, if Miss Caroline *does* play Fenella, it doesn't follow, as a matter of course, that she should think she has a pretty foot; and then such puppies as these young men are; he had the impudence to say, that –'

How far the amiable Mrs Porter might have succeeded in her pleasant purpose, it is impossible to say, had not the entrance of Mr Thomas Balderstone, Mrs Gattleton's brother, familiarly called in the family 'Uncle Tom', changed the course of conversation, and suggested to her mind an excellent plan of operation on the evening of the play.

Uncle Tom was very rich, and exceedingly fond of his nephews and nieces: as a matter of course, therefore, he was an object of great importance in his own family. He was one of the best-hearted men in existence: always in a good temper, and always talking. It was his boast that he wore top-boots on all occasions, and had never mounted a black silk neckerchief; and it was his pride that he remembered all the principal plays of Shakespeare from beginning to end – and so he did. The result of this parrot-like accomplishment was, that he was not only perpetually quoting himself, but that he could never sit by, and hear a misquotation from 'The Swan of Avon' without setting the unfortunate delinquent right. He was also something of a wag; never missed an opportunity of saying what he considered a good thing, and invariably laughed till he cried at anything that appeared to him mirth-moving or ridiculous.

'Well, girls!' said Uncle Tom, after the preparatory ceremony of kissing and how-d'ye-do-ing had been gone through – 'how d'ye get on? Know your parts, eh? – Lucina, my dear, act 2, scene I – place, left – cue – "Unknown fate", – What's next, ha? – Go on – "The Heavens –"'

'Oh, yes,' said Miss Lucina, 'I recollect –

"The heavens forbid
But that our loves and comforts should increase
Even as our days do grow!"'

'Make a pause here and there,' said the old gentleman, who was a great critic, in his own estimation, – '"But that our loves and comforts should increase" – emphasis on the last syllable, "crease", – loud "even", – one, two, three, four; then loud again, "as our days do grow"; emphasis on *days*. That's the way, my dear; trust to your uncle for emphasis. – Ah! Sem, my boy, how are you?'

'Very well, thankee, uncle,' returned Mr Sempronius, who had just appeared, looking something like a ringdove, with a small circle round each eye: the result of his constant corking. 'Of course we see you on Thursday.'

'Of course, of course, my dear boy.'

'What a pity it is your nephew didn't think of making you prompter, Mr Balderstone!' whispered Mrs Joseph Porter; 'you would have been invaluable.'

'Well, I flatter myself, I *should* have been tolerably up to the thing,' responded Uncle Tom.

'I must bespeak sitting next you on the night,' resumed Mrs Porter; 'and then, if our dear young friends here, should be at all wrong, you will be able to enlighten me. I shall be so interested.'

'I am sure I shall be most happy to give you any assistance in my power.'

'Mind, it's a bargain.'

'Certainly.'

'I don't know how it is,' said Mrs Gattleton to her daughters, as they were sitting round the fire in the evening, looking over their parts, 'but I really very much wish Mrs Joseph Porter wasn't coming on Thursday. I am sure she's scheming something.'

'She can't make *us* ridiculous, however,' observed Mr Sempronius Gattleton, haughtily.

The long-looked-for Thursday arrived in due course, and brought with it, as Mr Gattleton, senior, philosophically observed, 'no disappointments, to speak of'. True, it was yet a matter of doubt whether Cassio would be enabled to get into the dress which had been sent for him from the masquerade warehouse. It was equally uncertain whether the principal female singer would be sufficiently recovered from the influenza to make her appearance; Mr Harleigh, the Masaniello of the night, was hoarse, and rather unwell, in consequence of the great quantity of lemon and sugar candy he had eaten to improve his voice; and two flutes and a violoncello had pleaded severe colds. What of that? The audience were all coming. Everybody knew his part: the dresses were covered with tinsel and spangles; the white plumes looked beautiful; Mr Evans had practised falling, till he was bruised from head to foot, and quite perfect; and Iago was quite sure that, in the stabbing scene, he should make 'a decided hit'. A self-taught deaf gentleman, who had kindly offered to bring his flute, would be a most valuable addition to the orchestra; Miss Jenkins's talent for the piano was too well known to be doubted for an instant; Mr Cape had practised the violin accompaniment with her frequently; and Mr Brown, who had kindly undertaken, at a few hours' notice, to bring his violoncello, would, no doubt, manage extremely well.

Seven o'clock came, and so did the audience; all the rank and fashion of Clapham and its vicinity was fast filling the theatre. There were the Smiths, the Gubbinses, the Nixons, the Dixons, the Hicksons, people with all sorts of names, two aldermen, a sheriff in perspective, Sir Thomas Glumper (who had been knighted in the last reign for carrying up an address on somebody's escaping from nothing); and last, not least, there were Mrs Joseph Porter and Uncle Tom, seated in the centre of the third row from the stage; Mrs P. amusing Uncle Tom with all sorts of stories, and Uncle Tom amusing every one else by laughing most immoderately.

Ting, ting, ting! went the prompter's bell at eight o'clock precisely, and dash went the orchestra into the overture to 'The Men of Prometheus'. The pianoforte player hammered away with laudable perseverance; and the violoncello, which struck in at intervals, 'sounded very well, considering'. The unfortunate individual, however, who had undertaken to play the flute accompaniment 'at sight', found, from fatal experience, the perfect truth of the old adage, 'out of sight, out of mind;' for being very near-sighted, and being placed at a considerable distance from his music book, all he had an opportunity of doing was to play a bar now and then in the wrong place, and put the other performers out. It is, however, but justice to Mr Brown to say that he did this to admiration. The overture, in fact, was not unlike a race between the different instruments; the piano came in first by several bars, and the violoncello next, quite distancing the poor flute; for the deaf gentleman too-too'd away, quite unconscious that he was at all wrong, until apprised, by the applause of the audience, that the overture was concluded. A considerable bustle and shuffling of feet was then heard upon the stage, accompanied by whispers of 'Here's a pretty go! – what's to be done?' etc. The audience applauded again, by way of raising the spirits of the performers; and then Mr Sempronius desired the prompter, in a very audible voice, to 'clear the stage, and ring up'.

Ting, ting, ting! went the bell again. Everybody sat down; the curtain shook; rose sufficiently high to display several pair of yellow boots paddling about; and there it remained.

Ting, ting, ting! went the bell again. The curtain was violently convulsed, but rose no higher; the audience tittered; Mrs Porter looked at Uncle Tom, and Uncle Tom looked at everybody, rubbing his hands, and laughing with perfect rapture. After as much ringing with the little bell as a muffin boy would make in going down a tolerably long street, and a vast deal of whispering, hammering, and calling for nails and cord, the curtain at length rose, and discovered Mr Sempronius Gattleton *solus*, and decked for Othello. After three distinct rounds of applause, during which Mr Sempronius applied his right hand to his left breast, and bowed in the most approved manner, the manager advanced and said –

'Ladies and Gentlemen – I assure you it is with sincere regret, that I regret to be compelled to inform you, that Iago who was to have played Mr Wilson – I beg your pardon, Ladies and Gentlemen, but I am naturally somewhat agitated (applause) – I mean, Mr Wilson, who was to have played Iago, is – that is, has been – or, in other words, Ladies and Gentlemen, the fact is, that I have just received a note, in which I am informed that Iago is unavoidably detained at the post office this evening. Under these circumstances, I trust – a – a – amateur performance – a – another gentleman undertaken to read the part – request indulgence for a short time – courtesy and kindness of a British audience' – (overwhelming applause). Exit Mr Sempronius Gattleton, and curtain falls.

The audience were, of course, exceedingly good-humoured; the whole business was a joke; and accordingly they waited for an hour with the utmost patience, being enlivened by an interlude of rout cakes and lemonade. It appeared by Mr Sempronius's subsequent explanation, that the delay would not have been so great, had it not so happened that when the substitute Iago had finished dressing, and just as the play was on the point of commencing, the original Iago unexpectedly arrived. The former was therefore compelled to undress, and the latter to dress for his part; which, as he found some difficulty in getting into his clothes, occupied no inconsiderable time. At last, the tragedy began in real earnest. It went off well enough, until the third scene of the first act, in which Othello addresses the Senate: the only remarkable circumstance being, that as Iago could not get on any of the stage boots, in consequence of his feet being violently swelled with the heat and excitement, he was under the necessity of playing the part in a pair of common hessians, which contrasted rather oddly with his richly embroidered pantaloons. When Othello started with his address to the Senate (whose dignity was represented by, the Duke: a carpenter; two men, engaged on the recommendation of the gardener, and a boy), Mrs Porter found the opportunity she so anxiously sought.

Mr Sempronius proceeded:

'Most potent, grave, and reverend signiors,
My very noble and approv'd good masters,
That I have ta'en away this old man's daughter,
It is most true; – rude am I in my speech –'

'Is that right?' whispered Mrs Porter to Uncle Tom.

'No.'

'Tell him so, then.'

'I will. Sem!' called out Uncle Tom, 'that's wrong, my boy.'

'What's wrong, uncle?' demanded Othello, quite forgetting the dignity of his situation.

'You've left out something. "True I have married –"'

'Oh, ah!' said Mr Sempronius, endeavouring to hide his confusion as much and as ineffectually as the audience attempted to conceal their half-suppressed tittering, by coughing with extraordinary violence –

'true I have married her: –
The very head and front of my offending
Hath this extent; no more.'

(*Aside*) 'Why don't you prompt, father?'

'Because I've mislaid my spectacles,' said poor Mr Gattleton, almost dead with the heat and bustle.

'There, now it's "rude am I,"' said Uncle Tom.

'Yes, I know it is,' returned the unfortunate manager, proceeding with his part.

It would be useless and tiresome to quote the number of instances in which Uncle Tom, now completely in his element, and instigated by the mischievous Mrs Porter, corrected the mistakes of the performers; suffice it to say, that having once mounted his hobby, nothing could induce him to dismount; so, during the whole remainder of the play, he performed a kind of running accompaniment, by muttering everybody's part as it was being delivered, in an undertone. The audience were highly amused, Mrs Porter delighted, the performers embarrassed; Uncle Tom never was better pleased in all his life; and Uncle Tom's nephews and nieces had never, although the declared heirs to his large property, so heartily wished him gathered to his fathers as on that memorable occasion.

Several other minor causes, too, united to damp the ardour of the *dramatis personae*. None of the performers could walk in their tights, or move their arms in their jackets; the pantaloons were too small, the boots too large, and the swords of all shapes and sizes. Mr Evans, naturally too tall for the scenery, wore a black velvet hat with immense white plumes, the glory of which was lost in 'the flies;' and the only other inconvenience of which was, that when it was off his head he could not put it on, and when it was on he could not take it off. Notwithstanding all his practice, too, he fell with his head and shoulders as neatly through one of the side scenes, as a harlequin would jump through a panel in a Christmas pantomime. The pianoforte player, overpowered by the extreme heat of the room, fainted away at the commencement of the entertainments, leaving the music of *Masaniello* to the flute and violoncello. The orchestra complained that Mr Harleigh put them out, and Mr Harleigh declared that the orchestra prevented his singing a note. The fishermen, who were hired for the occasion, revolted to the very life, positively refusing to play without an increased allowance of spirits; and, their demand being complied with, they got drunk in the eruption scene as naturally as possible. The red fire, which was burnt at the conclusion of the second act, not only nearly suffocated the audience, but nearly set the house on fire into the bargain; and, as it was, the remainder of the piece was acted in a thick fog.

In short, the whole affair was, as Mrs Joseph Porter triumphantly told everybody, 'a complete failure'. The audience went home at four o'clock in the morning, exhausted with laughter, suffering from severe headaches, and smelling terribly of brimstone and gunpowder. The Messrs Gattleton, senior and junior, retired to rest with a vague idea of emigrating to Swan River early in the ensuing week.

Rose Villa has once again resumed its wonted appearance; the dining room furniture has been replaced; the tables are as nicely polished as formerly; the horsehair chairs are ranged against the wall, as regularly as ever; and Venetian blinds have been fitted to every window in the house, to intercept the prying gaze of Mrs Joseph Porter. The subject of theatricals is never mentioned in the Gattleton family, unless, indeed, by Uncle Tom, who cannot refrain from sometimes expressing his surprise and regret at finding that his nephews and nieces appear to have lost the relish they once possessed for the beauties of Shakespeare and quotations from the works of the immortal bard.

William Charles Macready

Theatre Review, The Examiner, *4 March 1843*

Much Ado About Nothing and *Comus*[15] were repeated on Tuesday to a crowded house. They were received with no less enthusiasm than on the night of Mr Macready's benefit, and are announced for repetition twice a week.

We are desirous to say a few words of Mr Macready's performance of Benedick; not because its striking merits require any commendation to those who witness it – as is sufficiently shown by its reception – but because justice is scarcely done to his impersonation of the character, as we think, by some of those who have reported upon it for that class of the nobility and gentry (not quite so limited a one as could be desired, perhaps), who seldom enter a theatre unless it be a foreign one;[16] or who, when they do repair to an English temple of the drama, would seem to be attracted thither solely by an amiable desire to purify, by their presence, a scene of vice and indecorum, and who select their place of entertainment accordingly.

There are many reasons why a tragic actor incurs considerable risk of failing to enlist the sympathies of his audience when he appears in comedy. In the first place, some people are rather disposed to take it ill that he should not make them laugh who has so often made them cry. In the second, he has not only to make the impression which he seeks to produce in that particular character, but has to render it, at once, so obvious and distinct, as to cast into oblivion for the time all the host of grave associations with which he is identified. Lastly, there is a very general feeling abroad in reference to all the arts, and every phase of public life, that the path which a man has trodden for many years – even though it should be the primrose path to the everlasting bonfire – must be necessarily his allotted one, and that it is, as a matter or course, the only one in which he is qualified to walk.

First impressions, too, even with persons of a cultivated understanding, have an immense effect in settling their notions of a character; and it is not heresy to say that many people unconsciously form their opinion of such a creation as Benedick, not so much from the exercise of their own judgement in reading of the play, as from what they have seen bodily presented to them on the stage. Thus, when they call to mind that in such a place Mr A, or Mr B used to stick his arms akimbo and shake his head knowingly; or that in such another place he gave the pit to understand, by certain confidential nods and winks, that in good time they should see what they should see; or in such another place, swaggered; or in such another place, with one hand clasping each of his sides, heaved his shoulders as with laughter; they recall his image, not as the Mr A or Mr B aforesaid, but as Shakespeare's Benedick – the real Benedick of the book, not the conventional Benedick of the boards – and missing any familiar actions, miss, as it were, something of right belonging to the part.

Against all these difficulties Mr Macready has had to contend, as any such man must, in his performance of Benedick, and yet before his very first scene was over on the first night of the revival, the whole house felt that there was before them a presentment of the character so fresh, distinct, vigorous, and enjoyable, as they could not choose but relish, and go along with, delightfully, to the fall of the curtain.

If it be beyond the province of what we call genteel comedy – a term which Shakespeare would have had some difficulty in understanding, perhaps – to make people laugh, then, assuredly, Mr Macready is far from being a genteelly comic Benedick. But as we find him – Signor Benedick of Padua, that is, not the Benedick of this or that theatrical company – the constant occasion of merriment among the persons represented in *Much Ado About Nothing*, 'all mirth,' as Don Pedro has it, 'from the crown of his head to the sole of his foot'; and as we find him, in particular, constantly moving to laughter both the Prince and Claudio, who may be reasonably supposed to possess their share of refined and courtier-like behaviour; we venture to think that those who sit below the salt, or t'other side the lamps, should laugh also. And that they did and do, both loud and long, let the ringing walls of Drury Lane bear witness.

Judging of it by analogy; by comparison with anything we know in nature, literature, art; by any test we can apply to it, from within us or without, we can imagine no purer or higher piece of genuine comedy than Mr Macready's performance of the scene in the orchard after emerging from the arbour. As he sat, uneasily cross-legged, on the garden chair, with that face of grave bewilderment and puzzled contemplation, we seemed to be looking on a picture of Leslie.[17] It was just such a figure as that excellent artist, in his fine appreciation of the finest humour, might have delighted to produce. Those who consider it broad, or farcical, or overstrained, cannot surely have considered all the train and course of circumstances leading up to that place. If they take them into reasonable account, and try to imagine for a moment how any master of fiction would have described Benedick's behaviour at that crisis – supposing it had been impossible to contemplate the appearance of a living man in the part, and therefore necessary to describe it at all – can they arrive at any other conclusion than that such ideas as are here presented by Mr Macready would have been written down? Refer to any passage in any play of Shakespeare's, where it has been necessary to describe, as occurring beyond the scene, the behaviour of a man in a situation of ludicrous perplexity; and by that standard alone (to say nothing of that mistaken notion of natural behaviour that may have suggested itself at any time to Goldsmith, Swift, Fielding, Smollett, Sterne, Scott, or other such unenlightened journeymen) criticise, if you please, this portion of Mr Macready's admirable performance.

The nice distinction between such an aspect of the character as this, and the after love scenes with Beatrice, the challenging of Claudio, or the gay endurance and return of the Prince's jests at last, was such as none but a master could have expressed though the veriest tyro in the house might feel its truth when presented to him. It occurred to us that Mr Macready's avoidance of Beatrice in the second act was a little too earnest and real; but it is hard dealing to find so slight a blemish in such a finished and exquisite performance. For such, in calm reflection, and not in the excitement of having recently witnessed it, we unaffectedly and impartially believe it to be.

The other characters are, for the most part, exceedingly well played. Claudio, in the gay and gallant scenes, has an efficient representative in Mr Anderson; but his perfect indifference to Hero's supposed death is an imputation on his good sense, and a disagreeable circumstance in the representation of the play, which we should be heartily glad to see removed. Mr Compton has glimpses of Dogberry, though iron was never harder than he. If he could but derive a little oil from his contact with Keeley[18] (whose utter absorption in his learned neighbour is amazing), he would become an infinitely better leader of the Prince's Watch. Mrs Nisbett is no less charming than at first, and Miss Fortescue is more so from having a greater share of confidence in her bearing, and a somewhat smaller nosegay in her breast. Both Mr Phelps and Mr W. Bennett deserve especial notice, as acting at once with great spirit and great discretion.[19]

Let those who still cling to the opinion that the Senate of ancient Rome represented by five shillings' worth of supernumerary assistance huddled together at a rickety table, with togas above the cloth and corduroys below, is more gratifying and instructive to behold than the living Truth presented to them in *Corialanus* during Mr Macready's management of Covent Garden, – let such admirers of the theatre track the mazes of the wild wood in *Comus*, as it is now produced; let them look upon the stage, what time

He and his monstrous rout are heard to howl,
Like stabled wolves, or tigers at their prey,
Doing abhorred rights to Hecate
In their obscured haunts of inmost bowers,[20]

– and reconcile their previous notions with any principle of human reason, if they can.

Speech for the General Theatrical Fund, 29 March 1847

I come now, gentlemen, to propose to you a toast which is uppermost, I dare say, in the thoughts of everybody present, which is 'the very head and front' of the occasion, and the cause which brings us together; which is, and ever must be, inseparably associated with the honour, dignity, and glory of the English stage; with its revival in splendour and magnificence from ruin and rubbish, with its claims to be respected as an art and as a noble means of general instruction and improvement. To whom could such a toast apply, if not to our chairman, Mr Macready? Of whom, gentlemen – so graceful and appropriate is the position he now occupies among us – I would say, if I may paraphrase what he knows well, that nothing in the Chair became him like the taking of it. It is as generous and true in him – at the head of his profession, and at the zenith of a proud and prosperous career, to take part with this Fund, and to be heard in this place urging its claims with a manly earnestness, because it is not restrictive, and because it does not favour a few, and because it addresses itself to the great body of actors, and most of all to those who most need it – as it must be of enduring service to the institution to receive such high and valuable testimony.

Gentlemen, it would be difficult for me to find terms in which to discharge the duty of proposing our chairman's health, in the difficulty I always feel as to the separation of his name from sentiments of strong personal affectation and attachment, if I were not happily relieved by the knowledge that, in your breasts as well as mine, the mere mention of Mr Macready's name awakens a host of eloquent associations, – like Hamlet, Macbeth, Othello, grey-haired Lear, Virginius, Werner, and a host of others, speak for him within us, like spirits.[21] We once again forget the encircling walls of his Covent Garden Theatre, or of Drury Lane – theatres then with nothing infamous to mock the lesson that the poet taught or shame the woman-student of it – and look upon old Rome, its senate and its army, or the Forest of Arden with its gnarled and melancholy boughs, or Swinstead Abbey Gardens with the cruel king upon his deathbed, or Prospero's enchanted island, or any of those scenes of airy nothing that he made plain and palpable. Oh! if one touch of nature makes the whole world kind, think, gentlemen, for how much of the kindred feelings that is amongst us tonight, or at any time, we are indebted to such an art, and such a man! May we be more and more indebted to him, year by year, for very many years to come! May we yet behold the English drama – this a hope to which I always cling – in some theatre of his own, rising proudly from its ashes, into new and vigorous existence. And may we, in the reception we now give his name, express all this, and twenty times as much; including the past, the present, and the future; and give him reason years hence to remember this occasion, with something of the pleasure and delight that we have through him derived from it ourselves! I beg to propose to you to drink the health of our chairman, Mr Macready.

Theatre Review, The Examiner, *27 October 1849*

Mr Macready appeared on Wednesday evening in *King Lear*. The house was crowded in every part before the rising of the curtain and he was received with deafening enthusiasm. The emotions awakened in the audience by his magnificent performance, and often demonstrated during its progress, did not exhaust their spirits. At the close of the tragedy, they rose in a mass to greet him with a burst of applause that made the building ring.

Of the many great impersonations with which Mr Macready is associated and which he is now, unhappily for dramatic art in England, presenting for the last time, perhaps his Lear is the finest. The deep and subtle considerations he has given to the whole noble play, is visible in all he says and does. From his rash renunciation of the gentle daughter who can only love him and be silent, to his falling dead beside her, unbound from the rack of this tough world, a more affecting, truthful and awful picture never surely was presented on the stage.

'The greatness of Lear,' writes Charles Lamb, 'is not in corporal dimension, but in intellectual; the explosions of his passion are terrible as a volcano: they are storms, turning up and disclosing to the bottom that sea – his mind, with all its vast riches. It is his mind which is laid bare. This case of flesh and blood seems too insignificant to be thought on; even as himself neglects it. On the stage we see nothing but corporal infirmities and weakness, the impotence of rage.'

Not so in the performance of Wednesday night. It was the mind of Lear on which we looked. The heart, soul and brain of the ruin'd piece of nature, in all the stages of its ruining, were bare before us. What Lamb writes of the character might have been written of this representation of it and been a faithful description.

To say of such a performance that this or that point is most observable in it for its excellence, is hardly to do justice to a piece of art so complete and beautiful. The tenderness, the rage, the madness, the remorse and sorrow, all come of one another and are linked together in a chain. Only of such tenderness, could come such rage; of both combined, such madness; of such a strife of passions and affections, the pathetic cry:

> Do not laugh at me;
> For, as I am a man, I think this lady
> To be my child Cordelia;

only of such recognition and its sequel, such a broken heart.

Some years have elapsed since we first noticed Miss Horton's acting of the Fool, restored to the play, as one of its most affecting and necessary features, under Mr Macready's management at Covent Garden. It has lost nothing in the interval. It would be difficult indeed to praise so exquisite and delicate an assumption too highly.

Miss Reynolds appeared as Cordelia for the first time, and was not (except in her appearance) very effective. Mr Stuart played Kent, and, but for fully justifying his banishment by his very uproarious demeanour towards his sovereign, played it well. Mr Wallack was a highly meritorious Edgar. We have never seen the part so well played. His manner of delivering the description of Dover cliff – watching his blind father the while, and not looking as if he really saw the scene he describes, as it is the manner of most Edgars to do – was particularly sensible and good. Mr Howe played with great spirit and Mrs Warner was most wickedly beautiful in Goneril.[22] The play was carefully and well presented, and its effect upon the audience hardly to be conceived from this brief description.

Two Views of a Cheap Theatre

As I shut the door of my lodging behind me, and came out into the streets at six on a drizzling Saturday evening in the last past month of January, all that neighbourhood of Covent Garden looked very desolate. It is so essentially a neighbourhood which has seen better days, that bad weather affects it sooner than another place which has not come down in the world. In its present reduced condition it bears a thaw almost worse than any place I know. It gets so dreadfully low-spirited when damp breaks forth. Those wonderful houses about Drury Lane Theatre, which in the palmy days of theatres were prosperous and long-settled places of business, and which now change hands every week, but never change their character of being divided and subdivided on the ground floor into mouldy dens of shops where an orange and half-a-dozen nuts, or a pomatum pot, one cake of fancy soap, and a cigar box, are offered for sale and never sold, were most ruefully contemplated that evening, by the statue of Shakespeare, with the raindrops coursing one another down its innocent nose. Those inscrutable pigeon-hole offices, with nothing in them (not so much as an inkstand) but a model of a theatre before the curtain, where, in the Italian Opera season, tickets at reduced prices are kept on sale by nomadic gentlemen in smeary hats too tall for them, whom one occasionally seems to have seen on racecourses, not wholly unconnected with strips of cloth of various colours and a rolling ball – those Bedouin establishments, deserted by the tribe, and tenantless, except when sheltering in one corner an irregular row of ginger-beer bottles, which would have made one shudder on such a night, but for its being plain that they had nothing in them, shrunk from the shrill cries of the newsboys at their exchange in the kennel of Catherine Street, like guilty things upon a fearful summons. At the pipe shop in Great Russell Street, the death's head pipes were like theatrical memento mori, admonishing beholders of the decline of the playhouse as an institution. I walked up Bow Street, disposed to be angry with the shops there, that were letting out theatrical secrets by exhibiting to workaday humanity the stuff of which diadems and robes of kings are made. I noticed that some shops which had once been in the dramatic line, and had struggled out of it, were not getting on prosperously – like some actors I have known, who took to business and failed to make it answer. In a word, those streets looked so dull, and, considered as theatrical streets, so broken and bankrupt, that the 'FOUND DEAD' on the black board at the police station might have announced the decease of the drama, and the pools of water outside the fire-engine maker's at the corner of Long Acre might have been occasioned by his having brought out the whole of his stock to play upon its last smouldering ashes.

And yet, on such a night in so degenerate a time, the object of my journey was theatrical. And yet within half an hour I was in an immense theatre, capable of holding nearly five thousand people.

What theatre? Her Majesty's? Far better. Royal Italian Opera? Far better. Infinitely superior to the latter for hearing in; infinitely superior to both, for seeing in. To every part of this theatre, spacious fireproof ways of ingress and egress. For every part of it, convenient places of refreshment and retiring rooms. Everything to eat and drink carefully supervised as to quality, and sold at an appointed price; respectable female attendants ready for the commonest women in the audience; a general air of consideration, decorum, and supervision, most commendable; an unquestionably humanising influence in all the social arrangements of the place.

Surely a dear theatre, then? Because there were in London (not very long ago) theatres with entrance prices up to half a guinea a head, whose arrangements were not half so civilised. Surely, therefore, a dear theatre? Not very dear. A gallery at threepence, another gallery at fourpence, a pit at sixpence, boxes and pit stalls at a shilling, and a few private boxes at half a crown.

My uncommercial curiosity induced me to go into every nook of this great place, and among every class of the audience assembled in it – amounting that evening, as I calculated, to about two thousand and odd hundreds. Magnificently lighted by a firmament of sparkling chandeliers, the building was ventilated to perfection. My sense of smell, without being particularly delicate, has been so offended in some of the commoner places of public resort, that I have often been obliged to leave them when I have made an uncommercial journey expressly to look on. The air of this theatre was fresh, cool, and wholesome. To help towards this end, very sensible precautions had been used, ingeniously combining the experience of hospitals and railway stations. Asphalt pavements substituted for wooden floors, honest bare walls of glazed brick and tile – even at the back of the boxes – for plaster and paper, no benches stuffed, and no carpeting or baize used; a cool material with a light glazed surface, being the covering of the seats.

These various contrivances are as well considered in the place in question as if it were a Fever Hospital; the result is, that it is sweet and healthful. It has been constructed from the ground to the roof, with a careful reference to sight and sound in every corner; the result is, that its form is beautiful, and that the appearance of the audience, as seen from the proscenium – with every face in it commanding the stage, and the whole so admirably raked and turned to that centre, that a hand can scarcely move in the great assemblage without the movement being seen from thence – is highly remarkable in its union of vastness with compactness. The stage itself, and all its appurtenances of machinery, cellarage, height and breadth, are on a scale more like the Scala at Milan, or the San Carlo at Naples, or the Grand Opera at Paris, than any notion a stranger would be likely to form of the Britannia Theatre at Hoxton, a mile north of St Luke's Hospital in the Old Street Road, London. The Forty

Thieves might be played here, and every thief ride his real horse, and the disguised captain bring in his oil jars on a train of real camels, and nobody be put out of the way. This really extraordinary place is the achievement of one man's enterprise,[23] and was erected on the ruins of an inconvenient old building in less than five months, at a round cost of five-and-twenty thousand pounds. To dismiss this part of my subject, and still to render to the proprietor the credit that is strictly his due, I must add that his sense of the responsibility upon him to make the best of his audience, and to do his best for them, is a highly agreeable sign of these times.

As the spectators at this theatre, for a reason I will presently show, were the object of my journey, I entered on the play of the night as one of the two thousand and odd hundreds, by looking about me at my neighbours. We were a motley assemblage of people, and we had a good many boys and young men among us; we had also many girls and young women. To represent, however, that we did not include a very great number, and a very fair proportion of family groups, would be to make a gross misstatement. Such groups were to be seen in all parts of the house; in the boxes and stalls particularly, they were composed of persons of very decent appearance, who had many children with them. Among our dresses there were most kinds of shabby and greasy wear, and much fustian and corduroy that was neither sound nor fragrant. The caps of our young men were mostly of a limp character, and we who wore them, slouched, high-shouldered, into our places with our hands in our pockets, and occasionally twisted our cravats about our necks like eels, and occasionally tied them down our breasts like links of sausages, and occasionally had a screw in our hair over each cheekbone with a slight thief-flavour in it. Besides prowlers and idlers, we were mechanics, dock labourers, costermongers, petty tradesmen, small clerks, milliners, stay makers, shoe binders, slop workers, poor workers in a hundred highways and byways. Many of us – on the whole, the majority – were not at all clean, and not at all choice in our lives or conversation. But we had all come together in a place where our convenience was well consulted, and where we were well looked after, to enjoy an evening's entertainment in common. We were not going to lose any part of what we had paid for through anybody's caprice, and as a community we had a character to lose. So, we were closely attentive, and kept excellent order; and let the man or boy who did otherwise instantly get out from this place, or we would put him out with the greatest expedition.

We began at half past six with a pantomime – with a pantomime so long, that before it was over I felt as if I had been travelling for six weeks, going to India, say, by the Overland Mail. The Spirit of Liberty was the principal personage in the Introduction, and the Four Quarters of the World came out of the globe, glittering, and discoursed with the Spirit, who sang charmingly. We were delighted to understand that there was no liberty anywhere but among ourselves, and we highly applauded the agreeable fact. In an allegorical way, which did as well as any other way, we and the Spirit of Liberty got into a kingdom of Needles and Pins, and found them at war with a potentate who called in to his aid their old arch enemy Rust, and who would have got the better of them if the Spirit of Liberty had not in the nick of time transformed the leaders into Clown, Pantaloon, Harlequin, Columbine, Harlequina, and a whole family of Sprites, consisting of a remarkably stout father and three spineless sons. We all knew what was coming when the Spirit of Liberty addressed the king with a big face, and His Majesty backed to the side-scenes and began untying himself behind, with his big face all on one side. Our excitement at that crisis was great, and our delight unbounded. After this era in our existence, we went through all the incidents of a pantomime; it was not by any means a savage pantomime, in the way of burning or boiling people, or throwing them out of window, or cutting them up; was often very droll; was always liberally got up, and cleverly presented. I noticed that the people who kept the shops, and who represented the passengers in the thoroughfares, and so forth, had no conventionality in them, but were unusually like the real thing – from which I infer that you may take that audience in (if you wish to) concerning knights and ladies, fairies, angels, or such like, but they are not to be done as to anything in the streets. I noticed, also, that when two young men, dressed in exact imitation of the eel-and-sausage-cravated portion of the audience, were chased by policemen, and, finding themselves in danger of being caught, dropped so suddenly as to oblige the policemen to tumble over them, there was great rejoicing among the caps – as though it were a delicate reference to something they had heard of before.

The pantomime was succeeded by a melodrama. Throughout the evening I was pleased to observe Virtue quite as triumphant as she usually is out of doors, and indeed I thought rather more so. We all agreed (for the time) that honesty was the best policy, and we were as hard as iron upon Vice, and we wouldn't hear of Villainy getting on in the world – no, not on any consideration whatever.

Between the pieces, we almost all of us went out and refreshed. Many of us went the length of drinking beer at the bar of the neighbouring public house, some of us drank spirits, crowds of us had sandwiches and ginger beer at the refreshment bars established for us in the theatre. The sandwich – as substantial as was consistent with portability, and as cheap as possible – we hailed as one of our greatest institutions. It forced its way among us at all stages of the entertainment, and we were always delighted to see it; its adaptability to the varying moods of our nature was surprising; we could never weep so comfortably as when our tears fell on our sandwich; we could never laugh so heartily as when we choked with sandwich; Virtue never looked so beautiful or Vice so deformed as when we paused, sandwich in hand, to consider what would come of that resolution of Wickedness in boots, to sever Innocence in flowered chintz from Honest Industry in striped stockings. When the curtain fell for the night, we still fell back upon sandwich, to help us through the rain and mire, and home to bed.

This, as I have mentioned, was Saturday night. Being Saturday night, I had accomplished but the half of my uncommercial journey; for, its object was to compare the play on Saturday evening with the preaching in the same theatre on Sunday evening.

Therefore, at the same hour of half past six on the similarly damp and muddy Sunday evening, I returned to this theatre. I drove up to the entrance (fearful of being late, or I should have come on foot), and found myself in a large crowd of people who, I am happy to state, were put into excellent spirits by my arrival. Having nothing to look at but the mud and the closed doors, they looked at me, and highly enjoyed the comic spectacle. My modesty inducing me to draw off, some hundreds of yards, into a dark corner, they at once forgot me, and applied themselves to their former occupation of looking at the mud and looking in at the closed doors: which, being of grated iron-work, allowed the lighted passage within to be seen. They were chiefly people of respectable appearance, odd and impulsive as most crowds are, and making a joke of being there as most crowds do.

In the dark corner I might have sat a long while, but that a very obliging passer-by informed me that the theatre was already full, and that the people whom I saw in the street were all shut out for want of room. After that, I lost no time in worming myself into the building, and creeping to a place in a proscenium box that had been kept for me.

There must have been full four thousand people present. Carefully estimating the pit alone, I could bring it out as holding little less than fourteen hundred. Every part of the house was well filled, and I had not found it easy to make my way along the back of the boxes to where I sat. The chandeliers in the ceiling were lighted; there was no light on the stage; the orchestra was empty. The green curtain was down, and, packed pretty closely on chairs on the small space of stage before it, were some thirty gentlemen, and two or three ladies. In the centre of these, in a desk or pulpit covered with red baize, was the presiding minister. The kind of rostrum he occupied will be very well understood, if I liken it to a boarded-up fire-place turned towards the audience, with a gentleman in a black surtout standing in the stove and leaning forward over the mantelpiece.

A portion of scripture was being read when I went in. It was followed by a discourse, to which the congregation listened with most exemplary attention and uninterrupted silence and decorum. My own attention comprehended both the auditory and the speaker, and shall turn to both in this recalling of the scene, exactly as it did at the time.

'A very difficult thing,' I thought, when the discourse began, 'to speak appropriately to so large an audience, and to speak with tact. Without it, better not to speak at all. Infinitely better, to read the New Testament well, and to let that speak. In this congregation there is indubitably one pulse; but I doubt if any power short of genius can touch it as one, and make it answer as one.'

I could not possibly say to myself as the discourse proceeded, that the minister was a good speaker. I could not possibly say to myself that he expressed an understanding of the general mind and character of his audience. There was a supposititious work-ing man introduced into the homily, to make supposititious objections to our Christian religion and be reasoned down, who was not only a very disagreeable person, but remarkably unlike life – very much more unlike it than anything I had seen in the pantomime. The native independence of character this artisan was supposed to possess, was represented by a suggestion of a dialect that I certainly never heard in my uncommercial travels, and with a coarse swing of voice and manner anything but agreeable to his feelings, I should conceive, considered in the light of a portrait, and as far away from the fact as a Chinese

Tartar. There was a model pauper introduced in like manner, who appeared to me to be the most intolerably arrogant pauper ever relieved, and to show himself in absolute want and dire necessity of a course of Stone Yard.[24] For, how did this pauper testify to his having received the gospel of humility? A gentleman met him in the workhouse, and said (which I myself really thought good-natured of him), 'Ah, John? I am sorry to see you here. I am sorry to see you so poor.' 'Poor, sir!' replied that man, drawing himself up, 'I am the son of a Prince! My father is the King of Kings. My father is the Lord of Lords. My father is the ruler of all the Princes of the Earth!' etc. And this was what all the preacher's fellow sinners might come to, if they would embrace this blessed book – which I must say it did some violence to my own feelings of reverence, to see held out at arm's length at frequent intervals and soundingly slapped, like a slow lot at a sale. Now, could I help asking myself the question, whether the mechanic before me, who must detect the preacher as being wrong about the visible manner of himself and the like of himself, and about such a noisy lip-server as that pauper, might not, most unhappily for the usefulness of the occasion, doubt that preacher's being right about things not visible to human senses?

Again. Is it necessary or advisable to address such an audience continually as 'fellow sinners'? Is it not enough to be fellow creatures, born yesterday, suffering and striving today, dying tomorrow? By our common humanity, my brothers and sisters, by our common capacities for pain and pleasure, by our common laughter and our common tears, by our common aspiration to reach something better than ourselves, by our common tendency to believe in something good, and to invest whatever we love or whatever we lose with some qualities that are superior to our own failings and weaknesses as we know them in our own poor hearts – by these, hear me! – surely, it is enough to be fellow creatures. Surely, it includes the other designation, and some touching meanings over and above.

Again. There was a personage introduced into the discourse (not an absolute novelty, to the best of my remembrance of my reading), who had been personally known to the preacher, and had been quite a Crichton in all the ways of philosophy,[25] but had been an infidel. Many a time had the preacher talked with him on that subject, and many a time had he failed to convince that intelligent man. But he fell ill, and died, and before he died he recorded his conversion – in words which the preacher had taken down, my fellow sinners, and would read to you from this piece of paper. I must confess that to me, as one of an uninstructed audience, they did not appear particularly edifying. I thought their tone extremely selfish, and I thought they had a spiritual vanity in them which was of the before-mentioned refractory pauper's family.

All slangs and twangs are objectionable everywhere, but the slang and twang of the conventicle – as bad in its way as that of the House of Commons, and nothing worse can be said of it – should be studiously avoided under such circumstances as I describe. The avoidance was not complete on this occasion. Nor was it quite agreeable to see the preacher addressing his pet 'points' to his backers on the stage, as if appealing to those disciples to show him up, and testify to the multitude that each of those points was a clincher.

But, in respect of the large Christianity of his general tone; of his renunciation of all priestly authority; of his earnest and reiterated assurance to the people that the commonest among them could work out their own salvation if they would, by simply, lovingly, and dutifully following Our Saviour, and that they needed the mediation of no erring man; in these particulars, this gentleman deserved all praise. Nothing could be better than the spirit, or the plain emphatic words of his discourse in these respects. And it was a most significant and encouraging circumstance that whenever he struck that chord, or whenever he described anything which Christ himself had done, the array of faces before him was very much more earnest, and very much more expressive of emotion, than at any other time.

And now, I am brought to the fact, that the lowest part of the audience of the previous night, *was not there*. There is no doubt about it. There was no such thing in that building, that Sunday evening. I have been told since, that the lowest part of the audience of the Victoria Theatre has been attracted to its Sunday services. I have been very glad to hear it, but on this occasion of which I write, the lowest part of the usual audience of the Britannia Theatre, decidedly and unquestionably stayed away. When I first took my seat and looked at the house, my surprise at the change in its occupants was as great as my disappointment. To the most respectable class of the previous evening, was added a great number of respectable strangers attracted by curiosity, and drafts from the regular congregations of various chapels. It was impossible to fail in identifying the character of these last, and they were very numerous. I came out in a strong, slow tide of them setting from the boxes. Indeed, while the discourse was in progress, the respectable character of the auditory was so manifest in their appearance, that when the minister addressed a supposititious 'outcast', one really felt a little impatient of it, as a figure of speech not justified by anything the eye could discover.

The time appointed for the conclusion of the proceedings was eight o'clock. The address having lasted until full that time, and it being the custom to conclude with a hymn, the preacher intimated in a few sensible words that the clock had struck the hour, and that those who desired to go before the hymn was sung, could go now, without giving offence. No one stirred. The hymn was then sung, in good time and tune and unison, and its effect was very striking. A comprehensive benevolent prayer dismissed the throng, and in seven or eight minutes there was nothing left in the theatre but a light cloud of dust.

That these Sunday meetings in theatres are good things, I do not doubt. Nor do I doubt that they will work lower and lower down in the social scale, if those who preside over them will be very careful on two heads: firstly, not to disparage the places in which they speak, or the intelligence of their hearers; secondly, not to set themselves in antagonism to the natural inborn desire of the mass of mankind to recreate themselves and to be amused.

There is a third head, taking precedence of all others, to which my remarks on the discourse I heard, have tended. In the New Testament there is the most beautiful and affecting history conceivable by man, and there are the terse models for all prayer and for all preaching. As to the models, imitate them, Sunday preachers – else why are they there, consider? As to the history, tell it. Some people cannot read, some people will not read, many people (this especially holds among the young and ignorant) find it hard to pursue the verse form in which the book is presented to them, and imagine that those breaks imply gaps and want of continuity. Help them over that first stumbling block, by setting forth the history in narrative, with no fear of exhausting it. You will never preach so well, you will never move them so profoundly, you will never send them away with half so much to think of. Which is the better interest: Christ's choice of twelve poor men to help in those merciful wonders among the poor and rejected; or the pious bullying of a whole Union-full of paupers? What is your changed philosopher to wretched me, peeping in at the door out of the mud of the streets and of my life, when you have the widow's son to tell me about, the ruler's daughter, the other figure at the door when the brother of the two sisters was dead, and one of the two ran to the mourner, crying, 'The Master is come and calleth for thee'? – Let the preacher who will thoroughly forget himself and remember no individuality but one, and no eloquence but one, stand up before four thousand men and women at the Britannia Theatre any Sunday night, recounting that narrative to them as fellow creatures, and he shall see a sight!

Speeches for the General Theatrical Fund

6 April 1846

Gentlemen, in offering to you a toast which has not as yet been publicly drunk in any company, it becomes incumbent on me to offer a few words in explanation, in the first place, premising that the toast will be 'The General Theatrical Fund'.

The Association, whose anniversary we celebrate tonight, was founded seven years ago, for the purpose of granting permanent pensions to such of the *corps dramatique* as had retired from the stage, either from a decline in their years or a decay of their powers. Collected within the scope of its benevolence are all actors and actresses, singers, or dancers, of five years' standing in the profession. To relieve their necessities and to protect them from want is the great end of the Society, and it is good to know that for seven years the members of it have steadily, patiently, quietly, and perseveringly pursued this end, advancing by regular contribution, moneys which many of them could ill afford, and cheered by no external help or assistance of any kind whatsoever. It has thus served a regular apprenticeship, but I trust that we shall establish tonight that its time is out, and that henceforth the Fund will enter upon a flourishing and brilliant career.

I have no doubt that you are all aware that there are, and were when this institution was founded, two other institutions existing of a similar nature – Covent Garden and Drury Lane – both of long standing, both richly endowed. It cannot, however, be too distinctly understood, that the present institution is not in any way adverse to those. How can it be when it is only a wide and broad extension of all that is most excellent in the principles on which they are founded? That such an extension was absolutely necessary was sufficiently proved by the fact that the great body of the dramatic corps were excluded from the benefits conferred by a membership of either of these institutions; for it was essential, in order to become a member of the Drury Lane Society, that the applicant, either he or she, should have been engaged for three consecutive seasons as a performer. This was afterwards reduced, in the case of Covent Garden, to a period of two years, but it really is as exclusive one way as the other, for I need not tell you that Covent Garden is now but a vision of the past. You might play the bottle conjuror with its dramatic company and put them all into a pint bottle. The human voice is rarely heard within its walls save in connection with corn, or the ambidextrous prestidigitation of the Wizard of the North.[26] In like manner, Drury Lane is conducted now with almost a sole view to the opera and ballet, insomuch that the statue of Shakespeare over the door serves as emphatically to point out his grave as his bust did in the church of Stratford-upon-Avon. How can the profession generally hope to qualify for the Drury Lane or Covent Garden institution, when the oldest and most distinguished members have been driven from the boards on which they have earned their reputations, to delight the town in theatres to which the General Theatrical Fund alone extended?

I will again repeat that I attach no reproach to those other Funds, with which I have had the honour of being connected at different periods of my life. At the time those associations were established, an engagement at one of those theatres was almost a matter of course, and a successful engagement would last a whole life; but an engagement of two months' duration at Covent Garden would be a perfect Old Parr of an engagement just now.[27] It should never be forgotten that when those two funds were established, the two great theatres were protected by patent, and that at that time the minor theatres were condemned by law to the representation of the most preposterous nonsense, and some gentlemen whom I see around me could no more belong to the minor theatres of that day than they could now belong to St Bartholomew fair.

As I honour the two old funds for the great good which they have done, so I honour this for the much greater good it is resolved to do. It is not because I love them less, but because I love this more – because it includes more in its operation.

Let us ever remember that there is no class of actors who stand so much in need of a retiring fund as those who do not win the great prizes, but who are nevertheless an essential part of the theatrical system, and by consequence bear a part in contributing to our pleasures. We owe them a debt which we ought to pay. The beds of such men are not of roses, but of very artificial flowers indeed. Their lives are lives of care and privation, and hard struggles with very stern realities. It is from among the poor actors who drink wine from goblets, in colour marvellously like toast and water, and who preside at Barmecide feasts with wonderful appetites for steaks,[28] it is from their ranks that the most triumphant favourites have sprung. And surely, besides this, the greater the instruction and delight we derive from the rich English drama, the more we are bound to succour and protect the humblest of those votaries of the art who add to our instruction and amusement.

Hazlitt has well said that 'There is no class of society whom so many persons regard with affection as actors. We greet them on the stage, we like to meet them in the streets; they almost always recall to us pleasant associations.' When they have strutted and fretted their hour upon the stage, let them not be heard no more, but let them be heard sometimes to say that they are happy in their old age. When they have passed for the last time from behind that glittering row of lights with which we are all familiar, let them not pass away into gloom and darkness, but let them pass into cheerfulness and light; into a contented and happy home.

This is the object for which we have met; and I am too familiar with the English character not to know that it will be effected. When we come suddenly in a crowded street upon the careworn features of a familiar face – crossing us like the ghost of pleasant hours long forgotten – let us not recall those features with pain, in sad remembrance of what they once were, but let us in joy recognise it, and go back a pace or two to meet it once again, as that of a friend who has beguiled us of a moment of care, who has taught us to sympathise with virtuous grief, cheating us to tears for sorrows not our own – and we all know how pleasant are such tears. Let such a face be ever remembered as that of our benefactor and our friend.

I tried to recollect, in coming here, whether I had ever been in any theatre in my life from which I had not brought away some pleasant association, however poor the theatre, and I protest, out of my varied experience, I could not remember even one from which I had not brought some favourable impression, and that, commencing with the period when I believed the clown was a being born into the world with infinite pockets, and ending with that in which I saw the other night, outside one of the royal saloons, a playbill which showed me ships completely rigged, carrying men, and careering over boundless and tempestuous oceans. And now, bespeaking your kindest remembrance of our theatres and actors, I beg to propose that you drink as heartily and freely as ever a toast was drunk in this toast-drinking city, 'Prosperity to the General Theatrical Fund'.

14 April 1851

I have so often had the gratification of bearing my testimony, in this place, to the usefulness of the excellent Institution in whose behalf we are assembled, that I should be really sensible of the disadvantage of having now nothing to say in proposing the toast you all anticipate, if I were not well assured that there is really nothing which needs be said. I have to appeal to you on the old grounds, and no ingenuity of mine could render those grounds of greater weight than they have hitherto successfully proved to you.

Although the General Theatrical Fund Association, unlike many other public societies and endowments, is represented by no building, whether of stone, or brick, or glass (like that astonishing evidence of the skill and energy of my friend Mr Paxton, which all the world is now called upon to admire,[29] and the great merit of which, as you learn from the best authorities, is, that it ought to have fallen down long before it was built, and yet that it would by no means consent to doing so), although, I say, this Association possesses no architectural home, it is nevertheless as plain a fact, rests on as solid a foundation, and carries as erect a front, as any building, in the world. And the best and the utmost that its exponent and its advocate can do, standing here, is to point it out to those who gather round it, and to say, 'judge for yourselves'.

It may not, however, be improper for me to suggest to that portion of the company whose previous acquaintance with it may have been limited, what it is not. It is not a theatrical association whose benefits are confined to a small and exclusive body of actors. It is a society whose claims are always preferred in the name of the whole histrionic art. It is not a theatrical association adapted to a state of theatrical things entirely past and gone, and no more suited to present theatrical requirements than a string of packhorses would be suited to the conveyance of traffic between London and Birmingham.

It is not a rich old gentleman, with the gout in his vitals, brushed and got-up once a year to look as vigorous as possible, and brought out for a public airing by the few survivors of a large family of nephews and nieces, who afterwards double-lock the street door upon the poor relations. It is not a theatrical association which insists that no actor can share its bounty who has not walked so many years on those boards where the English tongue is never heard – between the little bars of music in an aviary of singing birds, to which the unwieldy Swan of Avon is never admitted – that bounty which was gathered in the name and for the elevation of an all-embracing art.

No, if there be such things, this thing is not of that kind. This is a theatrical association, expressly adapted to the wants and to the means of the whole theatrical profession all over England. It is a society in which the word exclusiveness is wholly unknown. It is a society which includes every actor, whether he be Benedict or Hamlet, or the Ghost, or the Bandit, or the court physician, or, in the one person, the whole King's army. He may do the 'light business', or the 'heavy', or the comic, or the eccentric. He may be the captain who courts the young lady, whose uncle still unaccountably persists in dressing himself in a costume one hundred years older than his time. Or he may be the young lady's brother in the white gloves and inexpressibles, whose duty in the family appears to be to listen to the female members of it whenever they sing, and to shake hands with everybody between all the verses. Or he may be the baron who gives the fete, and who sits uneasily on the sofa under a canopy with the baroness while the fete is going on. Or he may be the peasant at the fete who comes on the stage to swell the drinking chorus, and who, it may be observed, always turns his glass upside down before he begins to drink out of it. Or he may be the clown who takes away the doorstep of the house where the evening party is going on. Or he may be the gentleman who issues out of the house on the false alarm, and is precipitated into the area. Or, to come to the actresses, she may be the fairy who resides for ever in a revolving star with an occasional visit to a bower or a palace. Or the actor may be the armed head of the witch's cauldron; or even that extraordinary witch, concerning whom I have observed in country places, that he is much less like the notion formed from the description of Hopkins than the Malcolm or Donalbain of the previous scenes.[30] This society, in short, says, 'Be you what you may, be you actor or actress, be your path in your profession never so high, or never so low, never so haughty, or never so humble, we offer you the means of doing good to yourselves, and of doing good to your brethren.'

This society is essentially a provident institution, appealing to a class of men to take care of their own interests, and giving a continuous security only in return for a continuous sacrifice and effort. The actor by the means of this society obtains his own right, to no man's wrong; and when, in old age, or in disastrous times, he makes his claim on the institution, he is enabled to say, 'I am neither a beggar, nor a suppliant. I am but reaping what I sowed long ago.' And therefore it is that I cannot hold out to you that in assisting this fund you are doing an act of charity in the common acceptation of that phrase.

Of all the abuses of that much abused term, none have more raised my indignation than what I have heard in this room in past times, in reference to this institution. I say, if you help this institution you will be helping the wagoner who has resolutely put his own shoulder to the wheel, and who has not stuck idle in the mud. In giving this aid you will be doing an act of justice, and you will be performing an act of gratitude; and this is what I solicit from you; but I will not so far wrong those who are struggling manfully for their own independence as to pretend to entreat from you an act of charity.

I have used the word gratitude; and let any man ask his own heart, and confess if he have not some grateful acknowledgments for the actor's art? Not peculiarly because it is a profession often pursued, and as it were marked, by poverty and misfortune – for other callings, God knows, have their distresses – nor because the actor has sometimes to come from scenes of sickness, of suffering, ay, even of death itself, to play his part before us; for all of us, in our spheres, have as often to do violence to our feelings and to hide our hearts in fighting this great battle of life, and in discharging our duties and responsibilities. But the art of the actor excites reflections, sombre or grotesque, awful or humorous, which we are all familiar with. If any man were to tell me that he denied his acknowledgments to the stage, I would simply put to him one question: whether he remembered his first play?

If you, gentlemen, will but carry back your recollection to that great night, and call to mind the bright and harmless world which then opened to your view, we shall, I think, hear favourably of the effect upon your liberality on this occasion from our Secretary.

This is the sixth year of meetings of this kind – the sixth time we have had this fine child down after dinner. His nurse, a very worthy person of the name of Buckstone,[31] who has an excellent character from several places, will presently report to you that his chest is perfectly sound, and that his general health is in the most thriving condition. Long may it be so; long may it thrive and grow; long may we meet (it is my sincere wish) to exchange our congratulations on its prosperity; and longer than the line of Banquo may be that line of figures which, as its patriotic share in the national debt, a century hence shall be stated by the Governor and Company of the Bank of England.

4 April 1863

Ladies and gentlemen, with my present responsibilities impending over me, I happened the other night, as I sat alone, to be reading a paper in *The Tatler* referring to the time when Mr Powell's company of performing puppets was in high vogue with persons of quality.[32] In that number of *The Tatler* the brilliant essayist gave a humorous description of a contest then raging between two ladies at Bath – Prudentia and Florimel – as to which of them should set the fashion to the greatest number of imitators. In the course of this noble struggle Florimel bespoke *Alexander the Great* to be acted by the players, and Prudentia bespoke *The Creation of the World*, to be acted by the puppets; at the same time darkly putting it about, for the confusion and ridicule of her rival, that the puppet Eve, whom I suppose to have been but indifferently modelled, would be found in figure 'the most like Florimel that ever was seen'. Now what were the missing charms, what were the defective points in this wooden lady's anatomy does not appear, otherwise I should have the honour of delicately stating them to this company; but it does appear that his Worship the Mayor inclined to the wooden side of the question, and that on high moral grounds he greatly preferred those innocent creatures, the puppets, to those wicked players.

Now, ladies and gentlemen, as I have a profound veneration for mayors and such like, this sentiment causes me to close the book and to consider how much we should gain if there were no manager now but Mr Powell, and if there were no actors now but puppets. In the first place – and on the immense advantage to be reaped here, I have no doubt we shall all be agreed – there would be no fund, no dinner, no chairman, and no speech. Then on Saturdays there would be no treasury, although I am told that that great point has occasionally been gained even under the existing system; there would never be any throwing up of parts, there would never be any colds, there would never be any little jealousies or dissensions; the two leading ladies might dress for any length of time in the same room without the remotest danger of ever coming to words, and the loftiest tragedian that ever was or ever will be, might be doubled up with his legs round his neck, and put away in the same box with the reddest-nosed and most flowered waistcoated of comic countrymen. Now these, I considered to myself, were the points to be gained. On the other hand there would be human interest to be lost, there would be the human face to be lost – which after all does stand for a little – and last, not least, there would be that immense amount of comfort and satisfaction to be lost by a large number of well-meaning persons, which they constitutionally derive from slightly disparaging those who entertain them. This last high moral gratification, this cheap, this complacent self-assertion I felt could not possibly be parted with; and, therefore, I quickly came to the conclusion that we must have those wicked players after all.

Ladies and gentlemen, it is an astonishing thing to me, but within my limited range of observation and experience it is nevertheless true, that there should be, and that there is, in a part of what we call the world – which certainly is in the main a kind, good-natured, always steadily-improving world – this curious propensity to run up a little score against, and as it were to be even with, those who amuse and beguile them. 'That man in the farce last night, made me laugh so much,' says Portman Square, Esq., at breakfast, 'that I hope there may be nothing absolutely wrong about him, but I begin to think this morning there must be.' 'My Dear,' says Mr Balham Hill to Mrs Balham Hill, 'I was so profoundly affected at the theatre last night, and I felt it so very difficult to repress my sobs when the poor mad King listened in vain for the breathing of his dead daughter, that I really felt it due to myself to patronise that gentleman this morning. I felt a kind of compensation to myself to regard him as an extraordinary man, having no recognised business that can be found in the Post Office Directory. I felt it necessary to put up with him, as it were, as a kind of unaccountable creature who has no counting house anywhere; in short, to bear with him as a sort of marvellous child in a Shakespearean go-cart.'

Ladies and gentlemen, this is quite true in a greater or less degree, I think, of all artists; but it is particularly true of the dramatic artist, and it is so strange to me. Surely it cannot be because he dresses himself up for his part, for, as you all know very well, there is an enormous amount of dressing and making-up going on in high stations all around us. I never saw a worse make-up in the poorest country theatre than I can see in the House of Commons any night when there is a message from the Lords; and I assure you, on my personal veracity, that I have known a Lord High Chancellor at twenty-five shillings a week who, in his wigs and robes, looked the part infinitely better than the real article at fifteen thousand a year. Ladies and gentlemen, I think the secret cannot lie here; I think the truth is that this little harmless disposition occupies a little quiet, out-of-the-way corner of our nature, and as I think it a little ungracious, and a little ungenerous, and certainly more so than it is meant to be, I always, whether in public or in private, on principle steadily oppose myself to it for this reason which I have endeavoured to explain to you. Although I am now going to urge upon you the case of, and am going to entreat your active sympathy with, this General Theatrical Fund on this eighteenth anniversary, you will hear from me nothing conventional about the

Poor Player
Who struts and frets his hour upon the stage,

which shall in any way separate him otherwise than favourably from the great community of us poor players, who all strut and fret our little hours upon this stage of life. His work, if it be worth anything to himself or to any other man, is at least as real and as hard to him as the banker's is to him, or the broker's is to him, or the professional man's to him, or the merchant's to him. His fund is a business fund, and is conducted on sound, business, honourable, independent principles. It is a fund, as many here already know, for granting annuities to such members as may be disqualified by age, sickness or infirmity from pursuing the theatrical profession, and also for extending aid to the sick, I think in some cases even when they are not members, and to the bereaved survivors of the dead. It is a fund to which the members contribute periodically according to certain carefully calculated scales, very often out of imperfect and very uncertain earnings. It is a fund which knows no distinction whatever of theatre, and knows no grade whatever of actors. I have had the honour of being one of its trustees from the hour of its first establishment, and I bear testimony with admiration to the extraordinary patience, steadiness, and perseverance with which those payments are made. Therefore, ladies and gentlemen, you will see that I occupy here the vantage ground of entreating you to help those who do really and truly help themselves, who do not come here tonight for a mere field-night and theatrical display, but who as it were rise to the surface once in every twelve months to assure you of their constancy and good faith and then burrow down to work again, many of them surrounded by innumerable difficulties, and, believe me, with little cheer and encouragement throughout the whole toiling year, and in obscurity enough.

Now, ladies and gentlemen, in defiance of all these heavy blows and great discouragement in the actor's life, I fearlessly add these words – if there be any creature here knowing a theatre well who knows any kind of place, no matter what, cathedral, church, chapel, tabernacle, high cross, market, change, where there is a more sacred bond of charitable brotherhood, where there is a more certain reliance to be placed on sympathy with affliction, where there is a greater generosity in ready giving, where there is a higher and more sacred respect for family ties, where there is habitually a more cheerful, voluntary bearing of burdens on already heavily burdened backs, then let him take his money out to that place, to me unknown, and not produce it here. But if he altogether fails in such knowledge, then let him communicate with Mr Cullenford,[33] now sitting expectant at a card table, and let him communicate to Mr Cullenford something to this fund's advantage, as he respects all the true saints in the calendar, and as he defies and despises all the sham saints out of it.

Now gentlemen, as I have taken upon myself to say what a good corporation the players are among themselves, and how cheerily and readily they invariably help one another, I may not unreasonably be asked by an outsider why he should help them. If it were the claims of an individual that I was advocating here in these days, I should be met, and very properly met, by the question, 'What is his case? What has he done?' Moreover, as to that agglomeration of individuals, the theatrical profession, we are most of us constantly met with by a reference to the times when there were better actors, and when there was a better stage literature, and with a mournful shrugging of shoulders over the present state of things. Now, accepting the theatrical times exactly as they stand, and seeking to make them no better than they are, but always protesting against anybody's seeking to make them worse, the difficulty with me standing before you is not to say what the actor has done, but to say what he has not done, and is not doing every night.

I am very fond of the play, and herein lies one of the charms of the play to me; for example, when I am in front – and when I discharge for the moment all my personal likings and friendships for those behind – when I am in front any night, and when I see, say, my friend Mr Buckstone's eye roll into the middle of the pit with that fine expression in it of a comically suspended opinion which I like so much, how do I know on whom it alights, or what good it does that man? Here is some surly, morose creature come into the theatre bent upon the morrow on executing some uncharitable intention, and the eye of Mr Buckstone dives into his right-hand trousers pocket where his angry hand is clenched, and opens his hand and mellows it, and shakes it in quite a philanthropic manner. I hear a laugh from my left – how do I know how many a lout has been quickened into activity by Mr T.P. Cooke's hornpipe? How do I know how many a stale face and heart Long Tom Coffin, and Nelson's coxswain, and Black-Eyed Susan's William, have come healthily dashing like the spray of the sea? Over and over again it is my delight to take my place in the theatre next to some grim person who comes in a mere figure of snow, but who gradually softens and mellows until I am also led to bless the face that creases with satisfaction until it realises Falstaff's wonderful simile of being 'like a wet cloak ill laid up'.

It is a joke in my home that generosity on the stage always unmans me, and that I invariably begin to cry whenever anybody on the stage forgives an enemy or gives away a pocket book. This is only another and droller way of experiencing and saying that it is good to be generous, and good to be open-handed, and that it is a right good thing for society, through its various gradations of stall, boxes, pit, and gallery, when they come together with but one great, beating, responsive heart among them, to learn such a truth together. Depend upon it, the very best among us are often bad company for ourselves (I know I am very often); and in bringing us out of that, and in keeping us company, and in showing us ourselves and our kind in a thousand changing forms of humour and fancy, the actor – all the solemn humbugs on the earth to the contrary not withstanding – renders a high and inestimable service to the community every night of his life.

I dare say the feeling peculiar to a theatre is as well known to everybody here as it is to me, of having for an hour or two quite forgotten the real world, and of coming out into the street with a kind of wonder that it should be so wet, and dark, and cold, and full of jostling people and irreconcilable cabs. By the remembrance of that delightful dream and waking; by all your remembrance of it from your childhood until now; and by your remembrance of that long and glorious row of wonderful lamps; and by the remembrance of that great curtain behind it; and by the remembrance of those enchanted people behind that; who are disenchanted every night and go out into the wet and worry; by all these things I entreat you to not go out into Great Queen Street by-and-by, without saying that you have done something for this fleeting fairyland which has done so much for us. Ladies and gentlemen, I beg to propose to you, 'The General Theatrical Fund'.

Notes

1. Both *The Maid and the Magpie* and *The Dog of Montargis; or the Forest of Bondy* were genuine dramas of the time, as are the other plays described at length by Dickens in this article.

2. The theatre visited here has been identified as the Royal Victoria (nowadays known as the Old Vic).

3. James Morrison was a controversial quack doctor of the time, frequently attacked by the medical professions and lampooned by caricaturists for his miracle cures.

4. The Britannia Saloon.

5. A deal in this instance meaning a pine board; the phrase 'deals in a timber-yard' is used on other occasions by Dickens.

6. H.F. Chorley's play *Old Love and New Fortune* was cancelled, despite a successful opening night, because he had not obtained the Lord Chamberlain's licence.

7. A short story in *Ingoldsby Legends* by R.H. Barham told of a Lady Hatton who sold her soul to the devil.

8. Andrew Ducrow was the proprietor of Astley's (as well as one of its performers).

9. Nankeen is a pale yellow cloth, whilst 'frogs' was used in the nineteenth century as a term describing both buttons and decorative tassels on an outfit.

10. Colley Cibber's adaptation of *Richard III* was so popular that throughout the eighteenth and nineteenth century it was thought by many to be the original by Shakespeare; it is Cibber's version, not Shakespeare's, that includes Henry's murder and the line 'Off with his head. So much for Buckingham'.

11. Stage right.

12. Sarah Siddons (1755–1831), the celebrated actress and sister of John Phillip Kemble.

13. The prompt-side wing, on stage left.

14. In D.F.E. Auber's opera, *Masaniello*, the eponymous hero, a Spanish fisherman, organises a revolt because the viceroy's son has taken advantage of his sister Fenella.

15. John Milton's masque *Comus* (1637) which was adapted by John Dalton in 1738.

16. A reference to the review in *The Morning Post*, which, among others, was not favourable of Macready's melancholic Benedick.

17. Charles Robert Leslie (1794–1859) was an artist who specialised in painting scenes and characters from fiction.

18. Mr Keeley played Verges.

19. Mrs Nisbett played Beatrice; Miss Fortescue played Hero; Mr Phelps played Leonato; it is not recorded who Mr W. Bennett played, but given his mention in reference to Phelps, it is likely to be Antonio.

20. *Comus*, Act II, lines 213–6.

21. Virginius is the title character in a play by Sheridan Knowles; Werner is the title character in a play by Lord Byron.

22. Henry Howe became a regular supporting actor to Macready, though the playbill offers no information on which character he played in the 1849 *King Lear*.

23. Samuel Lane (1803–71), the proprietor of the Britannia Saloon, initially made it a success through melodramas catering to the East End audiences; Lane demolished the building in 1858 and rebuilt it as the Britannia Theatre, adding respectability to its popularity.

24. Working in the stone yard was a form of labour undertaken by workhouse inmates.

25. James Crichton (1560–82), known as 'The Admirable Crichton' was celebrated posthumously for his wide-ranging talents and intelligence; Thackeray also referred to him in *Vanity Fair*.

26. John Anderson was a magician from Scotland who dubbed himself 'The Great Wizard of the North'.

27. 'Old Thomas Parr' was reported to have lived for 152 years between 1483 and 1635.

28. In *The Arabian Nights*, the Prince Barmecide lays on an imaginary feast for his guest.

29. Joseph Paxton (1803–65) was the architect who designed the Crystal Palace.

30. Matthew Hopkins was an infamous seventeenth-century witch-hunter, the self-proclaimed Witchfinder General.

31. John Baldwin Buckstone (1802–79), actor-manager.

32. Martin Powell was an eighteenth-century puppeteer with a taste for satire who is particularly associated with Punch and Judy.

33. William Cullenford, nineteenth-century actor, who played, among other parts, Ralph Nickleby in an adaptation of Dickens' *Nicholas Nickleby*.

Biographical note

Charles Dickens (1812–70), a true celebrity in the Victorian period, remains one of the best-known British writers. His most popular works, such as *Great Expectations* (1861) and *A Christmas Carol* (1843), continue to be read and adapted worldwide. In addition to fourteen complete novels, Dickens wrote short stories, essays, and plays.

At the age of ten, Dickens moved with his family from Chatham to London. Though his travels would later take him abroad, most notably to America, his permanent home remained in the city for the duration of his life. His early life was financially and emotionally unstable, and when his father was imprisoned for debt, he was sent to work in a blacking factory, an experience that haunted his later fiction. He worked as an office-boy and court reporter before his *Sketches by Boz* (1836–7) brought his writing to the attention of the publishing house Chapman and Hall. After the success of *The Posthumous Papers of the Pickwick Club*, Dickens was able to found the journal *Bentley's Miscellany*, and from then on all his major novels were published as serial instalments in his own magazines.

After more than twenty years of marriage, in 1858, Dickens abruptly separated from his wife Catherine, mother of his ten children, in order to pursue a relationship with Ellen Ternan, a young actress. He died suddenly in 1870, leaving his novel, *The Mystery of Edwin Drood*, unfinished.

Pete Orford gained his PhD from the Shakespeare Institute for researching the modern reception of Shakespeare's history plays. Since then he has become embroiled in an academic *ménage à trois* with Shakespeare and Dickens, presenting papers at conferences on both writers, as well as publishing articles and books. He is the general editor of *Divining Thoughts: Future Directions in Shakespeare Studies* and has edited two collections of Dickens' writings for Hesperus Press, *On Travel* (2009) and *On London* (2010).

HESPERUS PRESS

Hesperus Press is committed to bringing near what is far – far both in space and time. Works written by the greatest authors, and unjustly neglected or simply little known in the English-speaking world, are made accessible through new translations and a completely fresh editorial approach. Through these classic works, the reader is introduced to the greatest writers from all times and all cultures.

For more information on Hesperus Press, please visit our website: **www.hesperuspress.com**

SELECTED TITLES FROM HESPERUS PRESS

'on'

Author	*Title*	*Foreword writer*
Charles Dickens	*On London*	
Charles Dickens	*On Travel*	

Brief Lives and Classics

Author	*Title*	*Foreword writer*
Richard Canning	*Brief Lives: Oscar Wilde*	
Wilkie Collins and Charles Dickens	*The Lazy Tour of Two Idle Apprentices*	
Charles Dickens	*The Holly Tree Inn*	Philip Hensher
Charles Dickens	*The Wreck of the Golden Mary*	Simon Callow
Melissa Valiska Gregory and Melisa Klimaszewski	*Brief Lives: Charles Dickens*	
Melissa Valiska Gregory and Melisa Klimaszewski	*Brief Lives: Wilkie Collins*	